Scottish Histories

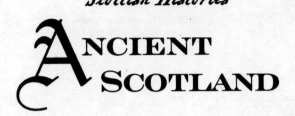

ANCIENT SCOTLAND

Also by David Ross
Scotland: History of a Nation
The Celts of the British Isles

Scottish Histories

Ancient Scotland

From the Roman Invasion to 1034

David Ross

WAVERLEY
BOOKS

For The Boys

Published 2008 by Geddes & Grosset,
David Dale House, New Lanark, ML11 9DJ, Scotland

Copyright © Geddes & Grosset 2004

ISBN 978 1 902407 68 5

Printed in India

Contents

Introduction

The outline of the land is recognisable straight away – the angular eastern coastline, the fretwork and crumbled fringe of sea lochs, headlands and islands on the west, that still form the familiar shape of Scotland today. The sea has encroached in some places and receded in others, but the differences in general outline are very small. Inland, though, the scene is quite different. We are looking at the landscape in the early decades of the first millennium of the Common Era, and the surface is mostly covered by thick forest, above which emerge the grassy or heathery upper slopes and, higher still, the crags and summits of mountain ranges not yet named, or whose ancient names are lost. For centuries now, the climate has been cool, wet and windy. Grey skies are normal; mist and low cloud are frequent; and, at ground level, it is a water-dominated landscape. The steely-grey surfaces of lochs and lochans, at different levels, glint among the trees, and thousands of smaller pools lie dark and hidden. Spilling down hillsides and spreading into marshes are streams and rivers, rougher and less controlled than those of the present day. Reeds, ferns, and rushes rise from marshy soil. Fallen trees and tangled branches lie in water or on damp earth, or have crashed on the hillsides. In many places, a carpet of thick woodland moss is starving the tree roots of oxygen and slowly killing the trees themselves. This climate and land surface are ideal for the formation of peat and, in open or cleared spaces, the peat bogs, imperceptibly but continuously, are consolidating and rising. In some parts the peat is slowly burying fields, piles of cleared stones, tree stumps, hut sites, and graves – the work of men and women.

For thousands of years, people have been living here. Their chopping, burning, and clearing have not yet made a great impact on the overall scene. A thousand years on, much of it will look very different. But on bay fronts and coastal headlands, in scattered woodland clearings, in circular frieze patterns along lochsides, on the high grassland in summer, the evidence of human habitation can be seen. Smoke rises from their fires; figures are at work in tiny fields or tending fishtraps in the estuaries. On certain hills and ridges, east and south, the outlines of earthworks can be seen, enclosing spaces, some of which are which are empty areas where flocks or crowds of people can be assembled, while others are filled by small round houses with pointed thatched roofs. Stone circles, massive burial mounds, long cairns, all of them already ancient, stand as witness to the skills and beliefs of earlier generations. A more contemporary style, castles for the living rather than for the dead, is seen in the dry-stone broch towers of west and north. Away from human communities, bears, wild pigs, wolves, and beavers live in the forest depths; the great auk and sea eagle dominate the multitudinous flocks of sea birds on the shores; elk and reindeer roam on the high moors. Human needs and wants take no account of their claim to a place and a part in this rich ecology – the process of their extermination is already well under way.

Trackless wilderness it may seem, but there is probably hardly a square kilometre of this landscape that has not been explored and investigated, assessed for what it can provide for its human masters, and claimed as the preserve of a particular group. They know the signs that hint at mineral deposits – copper, iron, silver, gold – and how to extract them and work them into tools, decorations, and weapons. Where coal crops out in heughs, they dig it out for their fireplaces. Some of this knowledge has been handed down from their forebears, some they have acquired through their own trial-and-error methods, and some has been passed on from other places. Communities hundreds of miles away by sea or land, are in regular or sporadic touch with them. As traders, people come and go; as settlers, perhaps, they come and stay. But even without the long-distance movement of people (and humans seem always to have been restless mobile creatures), news, ideas, and different ways of doing things spread, like moisture through branching twigs, across the edges of one community's area into the adjoining districts.

Though their far-off ancestors came as settlers after the ice age, these people by now are natives, aboriginals in a real sense: the nature of the land, its climate and seasons, have made a huge contribution to forming the routines and rituals of their way of life. Surrounded by space, with the riches of land and sea to live off, they have little to fear except the severity and shortages of winter – and perhaps one another, or the presence of ghosts and spirits. People speaking a language related to theirs, but at the opposite side of Europe, had told Alexander the Great that the only thing they were afraid of was that the sky might fall down. The encircling woods, the empty horizon of waters, the sense of immemorial possession, perhaps all have contributed to a sense of security. Rumours and news of far-off armies on the march, of empires, war, and conquests, may have seemed remote and irrelevant to their lives.

If so, they are mistaken. In the time of their great-grandparents, the distant southeastern corner of their island had been forcefully reconnoitred by a Roman general, Julius Caesar, and shock waves from that encounter had certainly travelled northwards. When their parents were children, the Romans returned to set up military bases in the south. Up here, they may still feel remote from such new threats, but they will not be disregarded. They are known about. Soon, they are going to be invaded.

CHAPTER ONE

The Year 78 and After

Pacification, Roman-style

In the early years of the Roman Empire, a provincial governor had to be soldier, statesman, and judge; and Gnaeus Julius Agricola, aged 38, newly arrived governor of the Roman province of Britannia in year 78 of the Common Era (CE), had spent his life in preparation for this role. He had had two energetic terms of previous service in Britannia, as a military tribune and a legionary commander, and had served as governor of the Gaulish province of Aquitania. It was customary that a governor should bring with him an informal group of friends and dependants as advisers and supporters, and to give him a little civilised company. Their incentive was usually the opportunity to make money through mineral concessions, farming, or import-export business. In Agricola's entourage was his new son-in-law, Gaius Cornelius Tacitus. Tacitus's special subject was rhetoric, the art of public speech. He had no particular role to play in the province's government, but employed his powers of observation and recording, and made notes for future reference. In 98CE, five years after Agricola's death, Tacitus published his biography of the governor. Written in order to praise and protect his father-in-law's reputation, it was also the first substantial account of life in the British Isles.

Britannia, by 78CE, comprised most of the present England and Wales, but the Roman province, inhabited by Celtic tribes with a tradition of warfare, was not at peace. The colony was still very new, founded only in 43. In 59, the large Iceni tribe, under their queen, Boudicca, had risen against the Roman occupation and been savagely put down. The tribes of Wales were still resisting. Agricola's first and immediate campaign was to consolidate the Roman hold by a ferocious, virtually genocidal campaign in north Wales, including the conquest of Môn (Anglesey), the centre of the Druidic cult. He then turned to the sprawling region inhabited by the tribe of Brigantes, which lay across the country from the Humber to the Wirral and up to the Cheviot Hills.

The Brigantes had earlier been seen as a friendly 'buffer state' between Britannia and the little-known peoples further north; but they had risen against Rome, had been defeated by Agricola's predecessor, and were now to be subjected to military occupation. Historians who note the benefits of Roman civilisation and its military efficiency usually pay little heed to the effects of the stupendous killing machine that was the Roman army. Its advance meant devastation, mass killings, rapes, torture, slave-taking and plundering: a nothing-barred terror campaign that was intended to stamp out all possibility of future resistance. In the year 80, arranged in two columns on the eastern and western sides of the country, building roads and forts as they advanced, the Romans pacified the Brigantes in their usual way and pushed on past the tribe's northern limits, encountering new tribal groups, until the columns converged in the area between the Forth and Clyde estuaries. Then, striking northeastwards, they reached as far as the River Tay. Agricola's tactics in these areas have been described as 'terrorising raids followed by offers of reasonable terms' (Frere, Britannia). In 81, he established a line of fortified camps south of the Tay, across the narrowest part of the country, between the firths of Forth and Clyde, and some distance north of where the Antonine Wall would later be built.

He stopped here because his instructions from the emperor Titus did not allow him to go further. Ever since Julius Caesar's time, the Roman government had taken care to ensure that provincial governors entrusted with armies did not exceed their orders. But Agricola had also reached a significant tribal frontier. North of the Tyne, in the Cheviots and Southern Uplands, he had encountered four large tribes. Latinising their names, Tacitus noted the Votadini on the eastern side; the Selgovae in the central area; the Novantae to the west, in what is now Dumfries and Galloway; and the Damnonii in Clydesdale. Of these, the Votadini became the most pro-Roman tribe, perhaps because they were under threat from the more numerous Selgovae. The Romans were adept at securing allies by exploiting such intertribal pressures.

These four tribes spoke a language now called Cumbric, very similar to the speech of the Brigantes; indeed the whole community of tribes in Britannia spoke what was essentially the same language, nowadays known as Brittonic. In the mountainous country to the north were numerous other tribes (13 were noted in this region by Ptolemy about 70 years later). They were not entirely unknown to the Romans. Even in 43CE, a delegation had come from far-off Orkney to offer its unasked submission to the emperor Claudius during his brief visit to the Roman headquarters at Colchester. This gesture may have been impelled by tribal warfare or other pressures of which we know nothing. But it is likely that there were greater differences between the southern and the northern tribes than there were between, say, the Votadini and the Selgovae. There was a language barrier. The northerners spoke a Celtic language closer to the Gaulish of continental Europe than to the Brittonic of the southern tribes. Despite the overture from Orkney a generation before, it seems clear that these northern tribes were hostile to the advancing Romans. Tacitus refers to the northerners as Caledones – hence the name Caledonia, which properly refers to the country north of the Tay – and describes them as physically different to the southerners: reddish-haired and large-limbed. He thought they resembled the Celtic tribes of Germany.

As they had lived unmolested, except by one another, for many generations, their hostility to the invaders was not surprising. In the ancient world, the fame of the Romans had spread far. While the Romans viewed themselves, at their best, as the bringers of peace, law, and civilised habits, the subject peoples saw them as ruthless killers, tax extorters, military press gangs, land-grabbers, slave-takers, and, above all, the arrogant imposers of an alien and unwanted rule. Thoughtful Romans, like Tacitus, were well aware of this perception, and he uses it skilfully when putting words into a Caledonian chieftain's mouth. In a celebrated phrase, the leader Calgacus is made to say that the Romans 'make a desert, and then call it peace'.

In 82, Agricola conquered the Novantae. They had already been sealed off by the new military road that ran northwards through Annandale, and by Roman control of the sea, and no major fort was built in their lands, though a fortified base was set up at Dalswinton, and a number of roads were built to ensure swift passage of troops. A Brittonic place name here, Penpont, 'head of the bridge', perhaps marks this work. It has been assumed that Agricola himself reached the Galloway coast, where an Irish chieftain came across to meet him. He was now master of the whole area south of the Forth-Clyde line, but the new emperor, Domitian, who had succeeded Titus in 81, instructed or empowered the governor to strike northwards; Tacitus implies that Roman valour and Roman glory would not allow less than a complete conquest of the British island.

Agricola made use of 'combined-operations' tactics, with a fleet off the coast supporting the army on the ground. Although the northerners also had ships, or boats, these are likely to have been of the curragh type, constructed of hide stretched over a wicker frame, lighter and lower in the water than the tubby wooden ships of a Roman fleet. Built for transport, not as fighting platforms, they were unsuitable for contesting the freedom of the sea. The composition of Agricola's fleet is not known: it could have included the heavy triremes, armed with catapults, that formed part of his Channel fleet, but the majority were probably smaller troop-carrying vessels and supply craft. Preparations for a major push went on through 83. The legionaries built forts to seal off the glens that opened on to their supply route coming up from south of Stirling into Strathmore. Even so, a serious attack was mounted by the northerners while the army was dispersed in three camps, with a surprise assault on the Ninth Legion, and only the rapid arrival of Agricola with his force avoided a damaging defeat. Not for the last time, the tribesmen, beaten but unsubdued, disappeared back into the Caledonian forest.

Fortified Camps and War Chariots

Right in the throat of the main pass leading north and west, at the strategically placed Inchtuthil, on the Tay near Dunkeld, Agricola set about the construction of a major fortress, large enough to provide the base for a full legion, around 5300 fighting men, plus substantial numbers of auxiliaries, administrators, and support personnel. Pre-Roman structures exist on the site and it may have been a Pictish strong point. No temporary encampment was intended here; although it was at the outer limit of Roman penetration, it would have been centrally placed once the anticipated conquest of Caledonia had been completed. Inchtuthil was not finished by the end of the campaigning season of 83, and work continued in 84. It was the biggest of the forts built at the orders of Agricola, or his successor in Scotland, some 40 in all, most of them following the main marching routes but some, like those at Drumquhassle and Bochastle, placed in outlying sites, which, to those who manned them, must have been wild in all respects.

The building of the great fortress, the raids of the Roman fleet far up the east coast, and the construction of military roads all showed the northern tribes that the Romans were in earnest. But the scale and pace of preparation also gave them time to mobilise their defence. The Selgovae's pattern of scattered small hillforts suggests a decentralised power system, making it easier for the invaders to overrun them. Either the Caledonians had a different system, with a stronger central power base, or they were able in the emergency to override the usual forms and unite themselves in a single large army.

A hundred and forty years before, the Gauls had united similarly behind Vercingetorix. While Tacitus makes it clear that the Caledonian army had a group of leaders, he gives pre-eminence to one by name, who has become 'the first historical Scotsman', Calgacus. Meaning 'swordsman', the name has an impersonal ring, like a title or sobriquet, but it is certainly a Celtic name. Once his base and supply lines were secured, Agricola's aim was to force a battle, and in 84 his army moved steadily northwards, round the flank of the Highlands and up into Aberdeenshire, its track marked by the still-traceable signs of speedily built 'marching camps', set up each night to provide security. The Caledonians must have seen a fight was unavoidable. The final part of the speech attributed by Tacitus to Calgacus reads:

'You are united: you Caledonians have never been slaves. From here there is no retreat by land, and even the sea offers no escape because of the Roman ships . . . Here you see a general, and an army; there you may see tribute-payments, work in the mines; with all the other calamities and curses that fall upon men who become enslaved. Whether these are to be imposed on us forever, or whether we avenge ourselves now for the attempt, will be decided here today. As you advance to battle, therefore, look back upon your ancestors, look forward to your posterity.'

Tacitus says the Caledonians assembled an army 30,000 strong. It included war chariots. Such items were obsolete elsewhere;

no Roman army had seen them for more than 100 years. The Caledonians were far behind the times; their isolated society no doubt had many other conservative aspects. With a Roman general's proper concern for Roman citizens' lives, Agricola placed auxiliary troops, including some recruited in Britannia, in the front line: 8000 of them, with 3000 cavalry on the flanks. The regular infantry, with four more cavalry regiments, were held in reserve. An exchange of thrown spears began the battle. Charging downhill, the Caledonians met the Roman centre and tried to spread around and envelop it, only to be swept back by the cavalry reserves. Several times the tribesmen rallied, but they could not break the armoured ranks, which cut them down each time they came on. Once again, the Roman army had demonstrated not only its invincibility but its virtual invulnerability against unarmoured opposition. Only 360 of them were said to have been killed, against an estimated 10,000 of the Caledonians.

The location of the battle, Mons Graupius, is still open to some debate, although aerial mapping of the Roman army's line of marching camps supports the long-claimed site by the hill of Bennachie, in Aberdeenshire, where there are Iron-Age fortifications, and at the foot of which a very large temporary Roman camp was built at Durno.

The fight took place relatively late in the campaigning season. Afterwards, the Caledonians withdrew rapidly from the battle zone. If they had a central headquarters, like the Votadini's *oppidum*, or walled fort, on Traprain Law, the Romans did not know of it. Agricola advanced further, perhaps as far as Forres, where he took hostages from an otherwise-unrecorded tribe, the Boresti, before leading his army south again. The fleet, or part of it, was sent to sail round the island of Britain, thereby establishing that it definitely was an island, and also noting the Hebridean archipelago. Contact was made with the Orkneys, whose inhabitants again surrendered to the Roman power, but not with Shetland, though the islands were seen from the ships. Orkney's repeated efforts to gain protection from Rome during the first century BCE suggest strongly that its inhabitants were under threat from the northern mainland or elsewhere or, at least, were pursuing a notably different policy to the mainland tribes.

Beyond the Limits of Empire

Agricola, after six years' service, was recalled to Rome. The opportunity to follow up his victory was denied him and not taken up by his successors. Instead of supplying the additional troops necessary to garrison the entire island, Domitian withdrew a legion to help with problems elsewhere along the empire's immensely long northern frontier. Tacitus's last comment is a bitter one: *perdomita Britannia et statim missa* – Britain was conquered, and then let go.

For the Caledonian tribes, assailed as never before, with a third of their fighting men left dead at Mons Graupius, it had been a terrifying demonstration of the empire's power and ability to strike deeply and destructively into their territory. Some historians see evidence in uncompleted hillforts as far north as Easter Ross that they had set about building new strongholds against the invasion. Nevertheless, no one emerged from the forests to bear their surrender or to treat for peace with the Romans. They were wise to wait. By late 86 or early 87, the great fort at Inchtuthil began to be dismantled before it had been fully completed. No legion could be spared to garrison it. Methodical as ever, the departing Romans buried a huge stock of more than 850,000 nails against a possible return. The cache of valuable iron was never found by the Picts, and was only unearthed in the 20th century.

Meanwhile, the Romans moved back behind the Forth-Clyde line, although some small forts in forward positions may have been maintained in service. The southern part of Scotland remained a zone under strict military control for nearly 20 years.

The forts at Newstead and Dalswinton were enlarged to hold substantial permanent detachments of infantry and cavalry. In 105, however, the Romans abandoned this territory also, apparently in the wake of a major uprising among the tribes, which caused the destruction of the two garrison forts and of several others to the south. The most likely reason for the withdrawal is a lack of manpower to withstand the scale of the attacks.

In Dacia (modern Romania), the emperor Trajan was leading a great campaign and had drawn substantial forces from the British garrison, including a complete legion. Now between the empire and the Caledonians there stretched a wide area occupied by the same tribes as before, the pro-Roman Votadini perhaps regretting their resulting exposure, the others jubilantly wrecking and burning whatever structures the departing troops left standing.

Twenty years on, in 125, the elaborate barrier of Hadrian's Wall was in the midst of construction. The emperor had come in person in 122 to inspect the frontier. It is not likely that Hadrian entered on what was to become Scottish soil – his visit was part of a tour of his remotest province, not a military expedition into the badlands. By 127, the barrier was complete from sea to sea, the most substantial frontier wall of the Roman Empire. None of the 76-mile structure lies in Scotland, but its importance to the country northwards was very great. Although a Roman area of influence lay to the north of it for many miles, the message was plain. It marked a political and military reality on both sides. It also served a regional tactical purpose in that it separated the Brigantes from the Selgovae and Novantae and prevented them from combining in hostilities against the Romans. These tribes had much in common, including language and culture, and their descendants would come together in the British kingdom of Strathclyde and its province or subkingdom of Rheged.

During this period virtually nothing is heard of the Caledonians. There are hints in the historical record that the province of Britannia was attacked from outside in the years

before 122 and the army was reinforced by 3000 men from
Spain and Germany in 122, the year in which Hadrian himself
visited the province. Such attacks were presumably from the
north. Picts of later centuries, in their king lists, produced a
series of names that, if authentic, go back as far as this time and
indeed earlier, suggesting the existence of a unified kingdom,
or at least of an overking. But scholars have all agreed that these
early names represent a blend of legend, imagination, and fab-
rication: although Calgacus and his fellow-leaders must have
had successors as heads of tribes or tribal groups, none can be
verified prior to the fifth century. In Caledonia, work on defensive sites stopped on, or soon after, Agricola's departure. The
Roman governors of Britannia maintained a force known as
areani or *arcani*, secret agents whose job was to move among the
northern tribes and report back on any dangerous developments; while their chief area of activity was among the
Selgovae and Novantae, it would be remarkable if they did not
penetrate further north. It may be partly from their maps and
reports that the list of tribes and places made by the Greek
geographer Ptolemy, at Alexandria, around 150, for inclusion in
his world atlas, was compiled, though some of Ptolemy's information was older and possibly already out of date.

Much reliance has been put on Ptolemy's list of tribes,
though it does not include Tacitus's Boresti, nor the Maeatae
and Attacotti, who are mentioned in later writings. It gives tribal
names in the mainland only, listing 13 to the north and west of
the Forth-Clyde line: the Damnonii, the Epidii, the Creones,
the Carnonacae, the Caereni, the Cornavii, the Smertae, the
Lugi, the Decantae, the Vacomagi, the Taezali, the Venicones,
and the Caledones (it remains unclear whether the latter was
the name of a single tribe or a collective name for all the tribes,
which is how Tacitus uses it). Two of these tribal names are
found elsewhere in Britain, the Damnonii in southwest England, and the Cornavii in Cornwall. Some may be totemic,
relating to an animal spirit, as with the Epidii, 'horse people'; the

Mull of Kintyre is Ptolemy's Epidion Akron, 'horse promontory'. There is very little correspondence between Ptolemy's
tribal names and later place names. On the Ross-Sutherland
border, the hill of Carn Sméart has been linked with the
Smertae, whose name may mean 'smeared ones' and, in Argyll,
very tentatively, Crinan with the Creones. The clearest links are
with the Caledones, found in three Perthshire names: Dunkeld
and Rohallion, both meaning 'fort of the Caledonians', and the
mountain Schiehallion, 'fairy hill of the Caledonians'.

These Caledonian tribes were, we have been told by generations of historians, barbarians. But what does this mean? To the
Romans, barbarians were people who were not Roman citizens,
who did not live under Roman law, who did not observe
Roman religion or other customs, and who did not wish to possess any of these advantages. Later, 'barbarian' would also equate
with 'not Christian'. In modern use, the word has gone further
downhill, with overtones of savagery, disorder, and primitivism;
the addition of 'hordes' quivers ready on the lips.

The natives of Caledonia were warlike, but so were the
Romans.

The Caledonians' reaction to Agricola's invasion in 84
showed that they were capable of order and unity. They lacked a
coinage, they lacked bathhouses (though they may have had an
equivalent in their 'burnt mounds'), and they lacked imperial
ambition. Their technology was inferior to that of the Romans,
though they had mastered ironworking and some of them were
accomplished workers in bronze. They decorated their bodies
in a way that, to the Romans, as it would to modern eyes, suggested a primitive wildness. They were skilled trackers, hunters,
and fishers, as well as pastoralists and farmers – country
dwellers with no concept of town life or how to establish it.
They kept animals – sheep, cows, pigs, dogs, and horses – and
lived with them, cheek by jowl. They made their own cloth and
clothes. Their way of life was close to the soil but not bound to
it – there was too much wild game to be caught for that to be

necessary. The agricultural seasons determined and measured the pattern of their existence. Having come to a certain under-standing of the universe, they lived their lives accordingly. They believed in the influences, baneful and benevolent, not only of a variety of gods or demigods, but also of local nature spirits. The reedy rippling tarn, the running river, especially at confluences, the silent oak grove, certain mountains, fertile fields – all were sustained by tutelary spirits, whom it was well to respect and placate. Often these spirits were conceived in animal form, and the present names of some streams and other features still reflect that association. The people had a class of priest-magicians but they used neither reading nor writing. Whatever they had of history, legend, lore, and records was committed to memory, as far as we can tell, since we know nothing of their use of tokens or symbols. In all these respects they were uncivilised, and some of these respects were maintained in the same countryside for almost 2000 years afterwards. There was one trait of civilisation that the Caledonians shared with the Romans: both communities employed slave labour. There were slaves, there were rulers, and in between was the bulk of the population, not as an undifferentiated multitude but each person incorporated into an established structure and system that was governed by duty, custom, ancestry, blood ties, and the loyalties of a kindred.

At different times, there is evidence of high artistic skill among the Caledonians. Long before the era of the Pictish sculptors, a tradition of high-quality ornamental metalwork emerged in the northeast of Pictland, between Aberdeenshire and Moray. This has been traced from the late first century – just about the time of Agricola's invasion – through to the second and third centuries. Bronze was the chief material, showing that the patrons could afford to import expensive tin for the smelting process. The armlets and bracelets often incorporate enamelled decoration in their terminals. Though it shows similarities with Brigantian work of the late first century, this work is sufficiently distinctive

to be termed 'Caledonian' by art historians. It is necessary to set
the notion of 'barbarian' aside in order to assess the Caledonians
and Britons from what we know of them. Social anthropology
has taught us respect for 'primitive' tribes of the modern era, and
their ability to preserve things we have lost. We should not be less
considerate of our own ancestors.

In the entire period of 1000 years covered by this book, there
was relatively little change to the basics of economic life. The
peoples north of Hadrian's Wall existed on a very different basis
from that which the Romans set up in their province to the
south. The Romans and Romano-Britons were town dwellers
whose economic life was based on the use of money in exchange
for goods and services, part of a firmly-imposed fiscal system that
applied the proceeds of taxation to the needs of government. In
many ways, though distorted by injections of plunder from conquest and by slavery, it was a market-based economy. Large
farms, with Roman-style villas as their headquarters, supplied
produce both for urban markets and for provision to the army.
The northern tribes, though they also acquired plunder and kept
slaves, had no such structure. They were country dwellers,
whose economic system had no need for money. The wealth of
the tribe and of its leaders was measured in agricultural terms,
chiefly in cows; the prestige of its leaders was measured in fighting men and in their own capacity for display and generous gift-
giving. Settlements needed to be self-sufficient for basic foods.
Their fields were small squares or rectangles of cultivated
ground where cereals, chiefly barley, and beans and early forms
of brassica were grown. The extent of such land and its defensi-
bility effectively limited the growth potential of the community.
Arable farming, pastoral farming – including the practice of tran-
shumance, with the annual removal of the animals and their
male and female attendants to upland pastures – and trapping,
fishing, and hunting, all with many supporting activities, were all
practised and must have taken up most of the community's time
and energy, even allowing for slave labour.

Among the Scots and the Britons (and probably the Picts), the social organisation was that of a kindred group, in which each person had a defined role and made a specific contribution. In return, each received a share of the tribe's produce and participated in its social activities and ceremonies. Some early 20th-century writers felt that this was a primitive form of communism, but there was nothing democratic about it; the tribal community was rigidly divided into groups whose status was fixed. Heredity (the fortune of being born into the right family), wealth, and the skill to manage and increase that wealth determined success. Fields and cows were owned by those who were of sufficient status, and were worked on behalf of the owner by those of lower rank and by slaves. The contributions of slave labour to the workforce, and of the sale of slaves to the rulers' wealth, are impossible to assess, but they may have been substantial. The upper ranks comprised warriors, who were required to own weapons and horses, and the 'professional' groups, who, in addition to bards and druids, embraced the skills of doctors, smiths, fine-metal workers, carpenters, shipwrights, and, in later centuries, stone-carvers and scribes.

In these communities, wealth flowed upwards. The splendour of the king or chief was the glory of his people or tribe. His riches were used for conspicuous display, seen at its most apparent in burials of the royal kin, in the tribute given to the gods, in the decoration of his house and the magnificence of his feasts, and in the opulence of his gifts. In addition to the produce of his own herds, flocks, fields, and fisheries, he was due a share of everyone else's. Although the claims on his own hospitality were very great, he was also entitled to claim the hospitality of his subchiefs: these ancient forms of taxation in kind, respectively known as 'kain' and 'conveth', lived on into medieval Scotland. The importance laid by the rulers on maintaining their due share was always great. Of the battle of Monith Carno in 729, between the rival Pictish kings Oengus and Nechtan, it is specially noted that among those killed were the *exactatores*, 'tribute collectors', of Nechtan (M. Anderson).

Underpinning this system, apart from the force of tradition, was the fact that it was in its essentials common to a set of neighbouring peoples. Its resilience and strength were shown by the fact that it survived alongside the very different economy and government of Roman Britain for more than three centuries, and lived on long after the Romans had gone. The later-coming Anglians and Vikings (though the latter were more commercially-minded) maintained social and economic systems that were broadly compatible. In the last resort, however, it was territory that mattered. The occupation and tenure of its land was the real guarantee of security to a tribe or a people. In the legends shared by Scots and Irish, the encounter of the Milesians with the triad of Ériu, Banba, and Fótla, goddesses of the land and soil, is a very significant one, confirming a potent bond between land and people; and we shall see that there are signs in place names of that bond having been imported to the landscape of Scotland.

From prehistoric times, there is ample evidence of contacts between the Atlantic communities and Celtic central Europe, and with the Greek, Etruscan, and Roman civilisations of the Mediterranean. Vitality was given by the trade of rare metal, chiefly tin, gold, and silver. In these exchanges, the territory of Scotland had relatively little to offer. There were no tin deposits. The Romans exploited the lead mines at Wanlockhead, where there was also silver to be found, but while they may have enriched the Selgovae and, later, the kings of Strathclyde, ores from here do not seem to have been exported. North Wales had richer lead deposits. Bog-ore deposits may have provided a limited amount of low-quality iron throughout the country. In *The Ancient Celts*, Barry Cunliffe writes:

> 'The material culture of Atlantic Scotland is limited and indigenous in the extreme, suggesting a high degree of

cultural isolation throughout most of the Iron Age [from around 700BCE into the Christian Era], though there is evidence of developing contact along the Atlantic seaways in and after the first century BC.'

This developing contact has been traced in the archaeological record at Dunadd in Argyll and it is believed that, by the fifth and sixth centuries, coastal fortified sites like this and Dumbarton were the main centres of such trade as there was. They were used as collection and distribution points. The outward traffic was probably chiefly in furs, especially white winter pelts, and in hides and feathers, pearls and semiprecious stones. Evidence of inward traffic can still be found in remains of pottery jugs and jars, and glassware. It has been suggested that wine was imported in barrels, which will not have survived; and other items, such as quality cloth garments, would also have perished. Imported goods then were transported inland, presumably in exchange for local products. Most of such material is found in the former Dàl Riada, with less of it in Pictland. No import-distribution centre to be compared with Dunadd has been found on the east coast. But, even in remote parts of Pictland, remains of imported objects have been found on domestic sites, from Roman glassware to jet ornaments.

The chief resources of Pictland were stone, wood, water, and space – enough of all these to allow for the establishment of viable settlements, but nothing to draw the interest of far-off capitalists, or to foster a vibrant economic life. At least until they were able to obtain blackmail payments from the Romans in return for peace, and later to plunder the rich villas of Roman Britain, the kings of the Caledonians were relatively poor. Such efforts as they could make towards the models of opulent display, as found in the 'elite' burial sites of the British tribes of eastern England, for example, would be modest, and help to explain the lack of such finds in Pictland (though factors such as the dampness and acidity of the soil may also have contributed to the decay of artefacts). It seems that a self-contained economic basis helped to preserve a culture among the Picts, particularly those of the far north, that was more archaic than that of the neighbouring peoples to the south and west. Old methods, old habits, and old customs are much more likely to remain, unchanged, in such a situation.

A New Frontier

Ten years after its completion, Hadrian's great wall was overrun for the first time from the north. Between 139 and 142 an energetic Roman governor, Quintus Lollius Urbicus, forced the tribes back and reimposed military rule on the area south of the Forth-Clyde line. By the year 143, Roman coins were struck to mark a victory in Britain. Despite the so-recent expenditure, and much modificatory work, on Hadrian's Wall, it was decided in that year to move the frontier line further north. Urbicus drafted men from three Roman legions to build a new wall, a short distance south of Agricola's old fort line, and named it in honour of the reigning emperor, Antoninus Pius.

The Antonine Wall, running 36 miles from Kinneil on the Firth of Forth to Old Kilpatrick on the Firth of Clyde, was a less ambitious structure than Hadrian's, but was still a massive barrier, 2.7m (nearly 9ft) high, 4.2m (14ft) wide at the base, 1.8m (6ft) wide at the walkway, built of turf on a stone base, and with 19 stone forts, further supplemented by watchtowers. It was fronted by a wide and deep ditch. The close spacing of manned posts shows that the wall was not merely a barrier but was used for observation and control, in a way that suggests there was a lot of movement around it and through its gateways. This would not always have been hostile – archaeological work shows increasingly that it is a mistake to view the Roman-Caledonian relationship as exclusively one of confrontation and warfare. While they kept a close lookout for any signs of militarism, the Romans, being businessmen, wanted to trade.

The northerners had wool, cows, and game: access to exotic wild creatures that the Romans enjoyed to hunt and eat, like auks and eagles, bear and boar. But the limited amount of Roman material from the first and second centuries found in areas north of the Antonine Wall suggests that the volume of such business was not very great. The Caledonians were not businessmen, traded only for what they needed, and were self-sufficient in most things. What they would have wanted most – modern iron weapons – the Romans were not likely to offer.

The Votadini, as the most 'Romanised' of the tribes, have left the greatest amount of Roman material to be found from this time, in their headquarters on Traprain Law in West Lothian. For the Romans, the great frontier walls were expressive of the fact that the territory to the north, though its people had much nuisance value, was of no commercial interest. Its conquest, other than to a glory-seeking emperor, was pointless. Antoninus was anything but a glory-seeking militarist, but in the early part of his reign, this northern extension may have been seen as the best way of establishing his imperial prestige. It is notable that he accepted the honour of a military triumph only once, and that was for the reconquest of southern Scotland. An interesting suggestion, made by Peter Salway in *Roman Britain*, is that the region north of the Antonine Wall may have been seen as a kind of military reserve, remote, dangerous, but not strategically vital, which could provide 'fighting experience to Roman armies and reputations to Roman officers'. To the inhabitants of Rome, even their province of Britannia was a remote and exotic place, beyond the 'ocean': Caledonia was a half-fabulous land about which wild tales could be told.

Despite the efforts to seal the northerners into their forest-clad territory, and despite periods of peace or truce that might continue for years, there was no sense that the frontier had settled, never mind the land beyond. The forts between the two walls remained fully manned at this time. It is likely that warrior groups from south of the Antonine Wall and even from beyond Hadrian's Wall moved discreetly north into the lands of the Caledones, bringing both their fighting strength and their anti-Roman zeal. Such groups may have come from as far away as Gaul.

If the Romans had their spies, the tribesmen also kept themselves informed about strategic events in the Roman province. The arrival of a new governor was usually taken as a chance to test his resolve. When the Brigantes rose against the Roman occupation, around the year 154, the frontier erupted into open and ferocious warfare. The trouble was serious enough for large reinforcements to be sent from Lower Germany, led by a new governor. It was more important for the Romans to retrieve the situation in the Pennines than that north of Hadrian's Wall; the troops were pulled back and the Antonine Wall abandoned. It was a humiliation for the imperial power, and the loss was made good as soon as possible. By 158 the Romans were back, manning the wall and the outlying forts to the north, as far north as Bertha, at the confluence of the River Almond with the Tay. But disturbances continued.

It is clear that the northern tribes tested the vigilance and speed of the Romans many times between 158 and 165. These tribesmen were the first to develop what John Barbour, the 14th-century poet of 'The Brus', referred to as 'Scottis weir', the preferred war tactics of Wallace and Bruce against military occupancy or invasion: sudden concentrated attacks and swift withdrawals, designed to harass a less mobile enemy. There is no account of a great pitched battle: one Mons Graupius had been enough. Yet the sequence of senior Roman generals in command, the moving up of cavalry units to Hadrian's Wall, and the refurbishing of the Wall itself, all suggest a powerful response to sustained and determined guerrilla-type warfare. Antoninus Pius died in 161 and his Wall ceased to be a matter of direct imperial prestige. Roman pragmatism could take over, and a new governor of Britannia, Calpurnius Agricola, implemented the decision to withdraw behind Hadrian's Wall around 165, though once again some outer forts continued to be garrisoned. The most notable of these was at Newstead, below the Eildon Hills, adjacent to what was or had been a stronghold of the Selgovae on the north hill. These forts also controlled access to the Votadini territory, and it is reasonable to surmise that the Votadini had remained faithful to whatever treaty or agreement they had had with the Romans, and both needed and deserved Roman protection.

Hadrian's Wall, following a topographically convenient line, did not reinforce a political or cultural boundary. Around 180, it was again stormed, probably at its central point, close to Corbridge, and the Roman writer Cassius Dio noted that a Roman general had been killed at the head of his army. Such actions, while the empire was still vigorous, merited, and received, large-scale and bloody reprisals. In the year 184, the governor Ulpius Marcellus began a campaign that may have extended as far north as the Tay; the emperor Commodus duly assumed the honorific title of Britannicus, indicating a Roman victory over the Britons. Following pacification, treaties were made, probably involving Roman subsidies to the chiefs in return for a nonaggression pact. For a few years there seems to have been relative stability but then, for ten years after 192, the situation deteriorated steadily. During this period of resumed raids comes, in 196, the first mention of the Maeatae. They appear to have been a confederation of tribes living in the central part of the country, 'next to the cross-wall that divides the island in half' (Dio). Some scholars have taken this to mean Hadrian's Wall; others the Antonine. In any case, they were established south of the Caledones, their name probably preserved in the hill of Dumyat, near Stirling, with its Iron-Age fortifications, and also in Myot Hill, not far away. The Maeatae are not the same peoples as the Caledones; Dio also describes the latter as a separate confederation, located beyond the Maeatae, sometimes working in alliance with them. The relationship between the Maeatae and the Selgovae and other southern tribes is not known, but as the former were not new arrivals, their name suggests either a new federation of tribes or simply the adoption by the Romans of a Celtic name for a group that they had previously known by a different name.

The hill peoples of west and north did not knuckle under to Roman rule. With 1/30 of the land of the empire, Britain required the presence of 1/10 of the Roman army. The three legionary centres were all close to the edge of upland country – York, Chester, and Caerleon. Such a force at his command made the governor a powerful figure. Between 192 and 196, the governor of Britannia, Clodius Albinus, was distracted from his task by his ambition to become emperor. Backed by his own three legions, he was accepted as a co-ruler by Septimius Severus, who had established himself as emperor at Rome with the support of 16 legions. But it soon became clear that Severus intended to be sole ruler.

The northern tribes must have followed rumours and reports of this imperial power game with keen interest. Late in 196, Albinus crossed to Gaul with an army; in February 197, he was defeated and killed by Severus. It seems that, whichever Wall was currently the frontier, it was still manned, as Britannia was not attacked. The Maeatae were unlikely to miss an opportunity to break through, if it had been available. But beyond the Wall, the new Roman policy of gifts to ensure peace had the disadvantage that the recipients of the gifts soon wanted more. Cassius Dio reported in 197 that the Caledonians had 'broken their undertakings'. We do not know what these undertakings were or what shifts of policy or power led to their being broken; but the consequences were bloody. Severus sent a new governor, Virius Lupus, to Britannia to restore Roman rule and order; Lupus had to contend with revolt in Wales and among the Brigantes, quite apart from the threatening behaviour of the Maeatae outside the province. He bought off the Maeatae, thereby restoring a buffer between Hadrian's Wall and the Caledones, and giving himself and his successors time to batter the Brigantes and the Welsh tribes back into submission. It was 206–7 before the Romans were able to start to restore Hadrian's Wall.

An Emperor Invades

Even while this action was being undertaken, the situation was deteriorating drastically. The contemporary Roman writer, Herodian, records that the governor, L. Alfenus Senecio, reported to Rome that the barbarians 'were in revolt, overrunning the country, carrying off booty and destroying most things'. The governor asked for reinforcements or – surely in desperation – an imperial intervention. Severus decided that the latter was preferable.

In the course of 208, the Maeatae and the Caledonians became unpleasantly aware that a full-scale imperial expedition was being mounted against them, with the gout-ridden 63-year-old Septimius Severus himself in command. The legionary centre of York was the base of operations, and preparations were made on a vast scale. Government of the empire was run from where the emperor was, and his court and chancery came with him, as well as substantial troop reinforcements. Dio says the emperor's aim was to subdue the whole of Britain, and Herodian notes that the northern tribes sent ambassadors down to York in the hope of making peace. But the imperial prestige required a victory. The accounts of Dio and Herodian become vague when it comes to describing Severus's actual campaign. Like Agricola's, this was to be a naval-military expedition, and Cramond, on the Firth of Forth, was established as a naval base and stores depot. The emperor's younger son, Geta, was left at York with the administration of Britannia, while the elder, Antoninus, better known to posterity as Caracalla, accompanied his father. A large fort, of around 9.7ha, was set up at Carpow, on the south side of the Tay estuary, and a bridge of boats was probably built across the river here. Camps were established along the line first traced by Agricola. If Severus wanted a battle, he had less success than

Agricola; the tribesmen stuck to guerrilla tactics, swooping down on detachments of Roman troops engaged in 'cutting down forests, levelling hills, filling up swamps and bridging rivers' (Dio). No doubt many heads were taken back to the warriors' homes; even a Roman writer talks of the army losing 50,000 men, though this is surely an exaggeration.

By the end of 209, Severus and his sons had the honorific Britannicus added to their names, though, apart from the fact that they needed to proclaim a victory to the Roman people, it is hard to see the justification. The line of Severus's camps goes up Strathmore, through the Howe of the Mearns and perhaps as far as Agricola had gone. The invasion and accompanying terror tactics were enough to force peace agreements on the tribes, and this was all the victory that Severus got. He returned to York. But in the following year the Maeatae again went on the offensive, though it seems the Caledonians at first did not. Severus resorted to the Romans' ultimate policy when faced with an intractable barbarian enemy. Himself very ill, he delegated Caracalla to lead a campaign intended to wipe out the Maeatae completely. Julius Caesar had set the pattern during his campaigns around 50BCE in Gaul, which are estimated to have cost the lives of a million of the inhabitants, and Agricola had employed similar tactics in Wales. This plan of annihilation appears to have brought the Caledones into the conflict in support of their southern neighbours. Then, in February 211, Severus died at York. Caracalla, still engaged in massacring the Maeatae, made some sort of accommodation with those whom he had been trying to exterminate, and hurried back to join in the struggle for supreme power.

Further campaigns against the northern tribes may have taken place in 211, but, back in Rome as emperor, Caracalla once again set Hadrian's Wall as the northern frontier. The total subjection of the island of Britain was set aside, to be seriously considered again only once, and that briefly, almost 100 years later, in 306. But for 50 years after the Severan campaigns, the Maeatae and Caledones were relatively quiescent.

CHAPTER TWO

Picts, Scots, and Others

The Gaels

As long before as 80CE, Agricola had stood on the Galloway shore and considered the conquest of Ireland. But the Romans ignored Hibernia as a potential colony or province. At the time of Severus's invasion of Caledonia, Ireland was inhabited by a large number of separate tribes. Each tribe, or *tuath*, was a unit under its own king, although they shared a common culture and language. Their speech was an early form of Gaelic. Although stemming from the same ancient original 'Common Celtic' language, Gaelic was in many ways different from the Celtic languages spoken on the east of the Irish Sea. It had not gone through the sound change of altering *qu-* to *p-* and, in other respects too, it was more archaic than the Brittonic speech.

Among the Irish tribes, the pattern of loyalties and identities was in constant flux. The leaders of stronger tribes, or groups of tribes, sought to extend their control over others, and this led to frequent warfare among the warrior caste. The concept of an 'overking' ruling several large groups forming a province, such as Ulster, had been established. But the later notion of an overall 'high king' did not then exist. Even the province was by no means a centralised kingdom. The overking's role was to arbitrate, to implement generally accepted laws, and to play an important part in priestly rites. One overking, around 210, was the famous and semilegendary 'Conn of the Hundred Battles', whose stronghold was in Meath, the central part of the island. The expansionist aims of Conn and his successors put severe pressure on the concentration of little kingdoms in Ulster, the northern province of Ireland. From the third century, refugees from tribal wars crossed the sea to settle in the underpopulated territory, whose extremities were only twelve miles away and easily visible from the land of the Dàl Riata people on the Ulster coast. Forming little Gaelic-speaking enclaves, and living – their chiefs at least – in the same sort of raths or duns they had known in Ireland, and probably still preoccupied by events in Ireland, they made little difference to the state of affairs in Caledonia. Bede, in his *History of the English Church and People*, refers to the first colonisation as taking place under a leader named Reuda, and there is an Irish tradition that Cairpre Riata led a migration to Argyll (or perhaps Galloway) as early as the third century.

It is plain that the inhabitants of northern Britain and Ireland were well aware of one another, and that colonisation from Ireland was taking place on a limited scale well before the traditional founding of Dàl Riada around 500. It would be likely that diplomatic gift-exchanging and intermarrying took place among kingly families on both sides of the North Channel, though there is no direct evidence from this time. Indications of links are found in some of the tales of the 'Ulster Cycle', centred on the site of Emain Macha, Navan Fort, in Ireland. Their greatest hero, Cuchulainn, was said to have learned the arts of war from a witch-warrior, Scáthach, who lived on Skye; and it was on another of these Amazons from the land of Alba, Aife (perhaps Scáthach by another name) that he first fathered a child. His own birth name, Sétanta, suggests a British origin, from the tribe of the Setantii. Further comings and goings between Scotland and Ireland are told in the celebrated account of 'Deirdre of the Sorrows', who escapes with her lover Nóise to an idyllic life in the neighbourhood of Loch Etive, until tragic destiny draws them back to Ireland, treachery, and death. The tales of Fionn mac Cumhaill and his band of poet-warriors would be brought over with the colonists, and remain so popular that their exploits would gradually be identified with the mountains and glens of the new homeland.

Picts' Houses

While the rath was characteristic of Ireland in the early centuries of the Christian Era, the inhabitants of Scotland lived in a variety of dwellings. Since at least 800BCE, the typical kind of house had been the 'roundhouse', circular, as its name implies, its walls built of wood or drystone, depending on the available materials. In the Hebrides, the far north, and the northern isles, the roundhouse was built of drystone, with relatively low thick walls and a pitched roof covered with turf or heather. Around 200BCE, it began to be built up into the distinctive form of the broch: a windowless circular tower, built of drystone without mortar. No broch has survived intact, and there is debate about whether they were two-storeyed or built with inner galleries round the walls. An inner shelf, or ring of ledge stones, known as a scarcement, has been found in many brochs. These could support either floor beams or a gallery; the latter is more likely since there was a central hearth on the lower level, and some provision would have to be made for the escape of smoke. At the top of the structure, a renewable movable roof may have been fitted. The internal diameter varied from 5m (15ft) to around 9m (28ft). The highest is likely to have reached 13m (43ft), estimated on the Broch of Mousa in Shetland, the highest broch remains still standing. Some brochs appear to have stood alone; around others were the houses of the chief's dependents, structures much more modest, even when built of stone, as at Gurness in Orkney, though these buildings may also have been built at a later time, when the broch was not in use as a chief's house.

When Agricola's fleet sailed round the Orkneys and Hebrides, the many coastwise brochs must have stood out dramatically, but no mention of these buildings is found in classical records. The earliest broch-type structures, mostly in the Western Isles but some on the western mainland, have double walls at ground level; later forms have massive single walls at ground level, becoming double above the base, and the narrow entrance passage is provided with a guard cell. The long narrow entrance passages – up to 3m (9ft) – sometimes combined with double doors, suggest that defence was a consideration for the occupiers. These differences have been used to group brochs in two general types. Since the building technique is believed to have begun in the Hebrides and spread north and east from there, the name 'Atlantic roundhouses' has been bestowed on brochs and duns (see below). Euan MacKie makes the point that the broch was used by peoples of differing material culture:

'The type of pottery and equipment found in the north mainland brochs contrasts in many ways with that from the contemporary sites in Orkney and even more with that from Shetland and the Hebrides.' (*The Dark Ages in the Highlands*)

The locations of more than 500 brochs have been identified. On the mainland, for the most part, they stand in regions inhabited by Ptolemy's Cornavii, Lugi, Smertae, Caereni and Carnonacae – tribes of whom virtually nothing is known, except that their names indicate a Celtic linguistic origin. However, it is clear that the northwest was not an empty zone. Ptolemy does not indicate names for the inhabitants of the Orkneys or Hebrides, but the remains of brochs show that they too were inhabited at this time. Even if not all these brochs were occupied simultaneously, their number indicates a sizable community (MacKie, an authority on brochs, was inclined to see all broch-building as within a period of about 200 years). Yet this vast northern region plays very little part in the known events of the following centuries, until the arrival of the Norsemen in the ninth century turned much of it into Viking territory. 'What went on north of the Great Glen was nobody's business,' commented Stuart Piggott in *Scotland Before History*. Undisturbed by invasion, and far from the frontiers, this abode of Pictish or pre-Pictish back-woodsmen must have been a substantial source of fighting manpower. Perhaps further archaeological work will establish more details about life and activity there in the long period of silence between the second and ninth centuries.

The imposing nature of the brochs has prompted suggestions that they were designed as much for ostentation as for practical defensive purposes. A number of writers have pointed out their inadequacy as 'castles'. Nevertheless, it is hard to avoid the view that defence was, at least, the initial purpose. Many brochs, like that of Gurness in Orkney, stand within fortified enclosures. One writer has referred to 'the apogee of the hedgehog principle' (W. D. Simpson, *The Stones of Scotland*). Stuart Piggott ascribed the Hebridean brochs to a movement of colonists from the mainland in advance of the threat of Roman invasion. But the brochs appear to have been mostly built well before the Romans were seen as a danger. In a society unused to external threats, where siege artillery was unknown, and in which there was a rit-ual of battle involving champions and warriors, rather than the population as a whole, in arms, the broch may well have offered sufficient security in which to round up the cows and the non-combatant tribespeople while the fortune of battle was tried among the fighting men. Architectural ostentation could have set in later, as with the towers of medieval Italy, still seen in Bologna and San Gimignano, whose function of combined security and display was perhaps not dissimilar to that of the brochs.

Hillforts

The era of the broch lasted perhaps 300 years. Around the year 100CE, the building of these structures came to a stop. Existing brochs continued to be inhabited in many cases, but MacKie also points to evidence, as in the harbour broch at Keiss, Caithness, of the structure being deliberately dismantled. Some brochs went on to be used for industrial purposes, as kilns, and others may have become storehouses. Often their stones were reused in new buildings on the same site or nearby. Much the same is true of the massive roundhouse structures built in the earlier centuries of the Iron Age. The new buildings that replaced them, as Sally Foster notes in *Picts, Gaels and Scots*, were smaller and less substantial in construction, even when built of stone. They form groups of single-family homes, in a pattern of new-style housing which seems to have spread across the entire country, Pictish and British, by the fourth or fifth century. Foster links this trend to the greater centralisation of government, with a consequent reduction in the importance of local chiefs or headmen. Just as medieval barons would require a royal licence to crenellate, so perhaps the regional chiefs were refused permission to inhabit fortified strongholds that could become bases of local insurrection. It is an appealing theory, but unlikely to be the whole answer.

In the regions we most confidently associate with Pictish power and population, and also in the Cumbric-speaking south, the broch scarcely exists. What we find are other kinds of structure. The most distinctive of these are hillforts. These defensive enclosures began to be erected on hilltops from about 800BCE, and most were built between then and 500BCE. They are most frequent in the south and east, and notably rare in the broch country. In area, they vary from large forts, like the Votadini centre on Traprain Law, which has been likened to the *oppidum*, or 'home town', of a Gaulish tribe, and the similar centre of the Selgovae on the north Eildon Hill, which shows the sites of about 300 houses, to small forts which could not hold more than a few family dwellings.

Three kinds of rampart construction have been identified. The most basic is simply a heaped-up line of stones, rubble, and turf. A more considered approach is seen in forts where the wall is faced with stone to make a more impassable barrier. The third type is the timber-laced wall, in which timbers have been inserted and joined together, to help create a more substantial and rigid barrier. This last sort has left questions of its own. Many such walls have been vitrified: that is, burning of the timber inserts has caused the stone to fuse into a ragged but solid mass. Discussion continues as to whether this was done deliberately by the builders or was the result of sieges. It has been pointed out that a vast amount of brushwood and piled logs against the wall would be necessary to make the sort of fire that would achieve such an effect, making the siege case less likely.

There are more than 100 examples of vitrified or partly vitrified forts. Vitrification as a defensive method might have been seen as a way of making it impossible to tear down a section of dry-stone wall to force an entry. All three construction methods seem to have been employed between around 700BCE and 300CE. Some forts appear to have been thrown up as a temporary expedient, like those around the head of the Moray Firth, which were begun on Agricola's invasion and abandoned, some of them only part-built, on his departure. Some important and more permanent forts were provided with more than one defensive line; in some of these 'multivallate' structures, like that of Barmekin of Echt, in Aberdeenshire, a progression can be seen from a triple-turf wall to a double-stone wall.

The intention behind the rampart-building is clear; less clear is whether all the forts were permanently occupied or whether some were simply places of assembly for religious observance or tribal gatherings, and refuges in times of war. For a cattle-owning society, they are mostly in highly inconvenient sites, especially so in the winter months. In the south, a region perhaps with a denser spread of population, and threaded by possible invasion routes, and where house sites have been identified within the walls, permanent forts may have been considered vital. They were certainly commanded by the leaders of society, as is clear from the valuables found at Traprain Law and other forts. It also seems to have been within the security of the stone or turf ramparts that the secretive and highly specialised skills of metalwork were practised. Bronze, gold, and silver were worked to produce a variety of artefacts and ornaments. Moulds have been found at numerous hillfort sites from Craig Phadraig, by Inverness, to Dunadd in the west and Traprain Law in the south.

Farmhouses, Duns, and Crannogs

On the whole, it seems likely that most hillforts were places of specialist function, and not used as residence sites for the whole tribal community. In the southern districts there are other sites, with defensive systems, but situated more accessibly for farming purposes. These are groups of roundhouses surrounded by a wooden palisade, usually small settlements of only half a dozen houses. The houses themselves were often stone-walled, with conical wooden roofs supported by wooden beams. Some of these dwellings were quite large, up to 19m (62ft) across, suggesting inhabitants of high status. A site at Hownam Rings, Roxburghshire – in the pro-Roman Votadini territory – is significant in showing several stages of defensive work in the centuries before the Romans came, from wooden palisade to stone wall, then to a multivallate fort, and finally, in the Roman period, losing its walls altogether and becoming an undefended site: both because the Roman protectors did not want other people's forts on their doorstep and because defence was not necessary, as long as the legions were there.

There are many other settlement sites where there is little or no evidence of defences, other than what might be necessary to keep tame livestock in and marauding animals out. Settlements of this kind occur not only in the 'protected' zone close to the Roman frontier, but far into the land of the Caledones in present-day Angus and the Mearns. It may be that the occupants of these dwellings moved into the hillforts at times of danger, but the undefended homes also suggest, at the least, periods of peace and a community whose main interests were agrarian – farmers rather than fighters.

Such people occupied the houses with 'souterrains' – long underground passages usually ending in a rounded cell – found from Sutherland to the Southern Uplands, and with examples in Lewis, South Uist, and Skye (Foster, 16), but most concentrated in Angus, Kincardineshire, and Fife. These too, in their time, have been regarded as uniquely 'Pictish', but they go back in time hundreds of years before the historical Picts, and there are examples of comparable structures in Ireland. Souterrains were still being built after the departure of the Romans: a Roman lintel was found built into one at Crichton, Midlothian. Many of the souterrains in Angus and Perthshire were filled up and put out of use in the second or third century BCE, for reasons not fully understood; and souterrains do not appear to have been dug by the historical Picts. Dr Richard Feachem wrote in *North Britons* that they 'exhibit no signs that they were ever occupied by man or beast, and in spite of all the work done on them, their purpose remains a mystery.'

Nowadays, archaeologists see them as storage places rather than dwellings, though they were possibly also used for ritual purposes linked with harvest and food preservation. Such practices would have been seen as protective and preservative – it would be many centuries before science began to detach itself from cult- and myth-based belief. The houses built above or beside the souterrains, of stone or wood, have long been destroyed but aerial photography shows their form: typically a two-cell structure like a figure – of eight. Many such houses show evidence of having had a scooped-out floor, with the possibility that there was a 'cellar' space under the floor, though they simply have been semisubterranean dwellings. It is quite possible that the souterrain stores, which must have been subject to water incursions and to infestation by rats and mice, were replaced by overground wooden barns, perhaps with floors raised on stone or wood blocks, whose remains would be very hard to trace.

Two other types of larger house, the dun and the crannog, though less showy than the broch and much smaller than the hillfort, had a longer life than either as living places for both Caledonians and Scots, and provided living quarters for a greater number of people. The classic dun is a stone-walled fort of circular or near-circular shape. It might range from 6m (18ft) to around 20m (63ft) at its widest. The larger ones probably incorporated several houses; the smaller ones, very much the majority, had a single overall roof. Found in greatest numbers in Argyll and more thinly spread to north and south on the west coast, the dun has been seen as a Scottish import from Ireland, where they are very common. The walls of some larger duns were reinforced with timber beams, as many hillfort walls were, though there is no recorded evidence of 'vitrified' duns.

Lake dwellings have a long pedigree in human history and the Scottish crannog goes back far into the first millennium BCE, and perhaps further. It had numerous advantages. Built of wood on a base frame of large timbers, crannogs were placed on natural or artificial islands in inland lochs or on shallow tidal beaches, and joined to the land by a causeway that could be partly lifted to isolate the site. Seashore crannogs would have rock breakwaters to mitigate the erosive and destructive action of tides and waves. There were two types: while crannogs in the Highland area are usually based on artificial mounds of stone, those to the south appear to be raised on platforms of timber, brushwood, and peat. Crannogs were occupied through the first millennium CE and into medieval times. Among their advantages were access to food in the form of fish and water birds, and to water. Their main hazard was fire, but this applied also to the thatched roofs of stone buildings on land. Crannogs were built throughout the mainland and Western Isles; remains have been found in Kirkcudbrightshire and in Sutherland; the Perthshire lochs appear to have been fringed by crannog dwellers, and numerous loch sites in Angus and Aberdeenshire have also been identified.

Crannogs could be quite substantial, with a diameter of up to 20m (63ft), and it has been surmised that they were, at least when first constructed, the dwellings of high-status persons. Dr Richard Feachem noted that:

> 'The inhabitants of crannogs had the use of dug-out canoes and possibly also of carvel-built [flush-planked] canoes, several of which have been found close to crannog islands . . . When the docks at Glasgow were being built during the nineteenth century no fewer than 26 canoes of various kinds were uncovered and recorded . . . an indication that there may have been a settlement of crannogs, and other mere-houses, of considerable size and importance in the heart of the present city of Glasgow, a damp Damnonian predecessor of the modern metropolis.' (*North Britons*)

Little is known for certain about the status of the inhabitants of these dwellings, or the structure of their communities. Where dun and crannog are both found, was the type of residence a matter of choice or did it define social status within the tribe; or even demarcate different tribal traditions that continued to co-exist? If so, who controlled whom? Where, within these settlements, did the slaves live? Particularly in northern Pictland, these questions have no certain answer. The distribution of brochs and the lack of hillforts in this region suggest a society that had no established central authority, but was rather a congregation of independent tribes, each in its own defined area. Such a society was normally vulnerable to attack, since it had no systems for unified action. But no evidence of attack has been found.

It has been suggested that the hillforts in the northeastern coastland, like that on Knockfarrel above Strathpeffer, may have been set up as defences against the broch-building northerners, and thus mark some sort of a frontier. Euan MacKie, in showing that the hillforts went up long before the brochs, disproves this defensive notion. In noting that the artefacts found in Caithness and Sutherland brochs show that 'this material culture is much more closely allied to that of the eastern mainland between the Moray Firth and the Firth of Forth than to that of the brochs in the rest of the Atlantic province', he infers that the northerners had much in common with the southern Picts. Once again, too, the difference of Orkney and Shetland is apparent.

Smaller individual or grouped buildings have been found in a variation of shapes and sizes. A gradual change took place in building style and material and, by around 500CE, instead of the large rounded structures of earlier settlements, timber buildings of rectangular or near-rectangular form began to be built in southern Pictland. In areas where stone was more accessible than timber, like Caithness and Orkney, stone houses continued to be built, often of the figure-of-eight shape, but also of 'shamrock' shape, where a central area with the fire, under the highest part of the roof, was ringed by several compartments, some of which seem to have been used for storage. Stone tanks in these compartments may have kept drinking water or live crabs and lobsters.

Houses of the first millennium CE are often found built over or against the middens of dwellings dating from the New Stone Age, 1000 years or more before, and indicating lengthy human occupancy of desirable sites. The change from circular to rectangular homes was prompted by unknown factors. Stuart Piggott noted in *Scotland Before History* that:

'The circumstances of the adoption throughout Scotland of the rectangular house (in its simplest form as represented by a 'black house') form one of the outstanding unresolved problems in northern archaeology.'

Euan MacKie notes at Forss in Caithness the most unusual existence of two stone long houses, and suggests these show the arrival of Iron-Age people from the continent, where such houses were built by several cultural groups 'in the not distant past' (*The Dark Ages in the Highlands*). In most respects, there is not much difference between these early medieval houses and the classic 'black houses' inhabited in various parts of the far north and the Hebrides until far into the 19th century. While it may not say much for 'progress' not to have got round to installing a fireplace and chimney by 1850, it says a great deal for cultural continuity.

Another Emperor Invades

Through most of the third century, the tribes north of Hadrian's Wall lapse from recorded (i.e. Roman) history. When they reappear, it is in response to developments south of the Wall. Here, the old province had been reorganised into two, Britannia Superior as the southern one, with legionary bases at Chester and Caerleon, and its commercial and administrative centre at London; and Britannia Inferior, the northern province, with its legionary and administrative centre at York. From 260, the northwest part of the empire, including Britannia, was ruled as a separate breakaway entity, the 'Gallic Empire', by three successive military emperors, until Aurelian restored central rule in 274. In the year 285, the recently-acceded emperor Diocletian assumed Britannicus Maximus as one of his titles. The implication of this is that a Roman military victory of some scale over British tribes had occurred, but we do not know where it happened or who was defeated. Between 287 and 296, under two successive military leaders, Britannia's provinces were again detached from the central rule of Rome, forming part of a separate but still Roman empire. These leaders, Carausius and his assassin and successor, Allectus, had to contend with the slow but inevitable response of the empire proper and, faced with the need to fight on the continent or face invasion on the south coast, would naturally try to secure their northern frontier by a treaty with the tribes.

It seems that there was relatively little opportunist raiding across the Wall in 296–7, despite the withdrawal of frontier troops. In 297, an imperial army landed and defeated Allectus; Britannia was again restored to the empire. A Roman panegyric, or praise composition, of this year, hardly the most reliable of historical texts, records that even the northernmost peoples of the island were obedient to Constantius, the Caesar, or junior co-emperor, of the West.

In 306, Constantius, now a full Augustus, or senior co-emperor, embarked on a campaign across Hadrian's Wall. The reasons for this invasion are not altogether clear. The 'obedience' of 297, if it existed, seems to have evaporated. A possible explanation is that the tribes had colluded with Carausius and Allectus, and so were deemed to require punishment. A Latin panegyrist of around 310 denied a 'popular belief' that Constantius had simply wanted to earn the glory of a military victory, and put the reason down to the divine summons to Rome to reach *intimum terrarum limen*, the very end of the earth.

Enter the Picts

Little is known of this campaign in detail, except that the enemy encountered by Constantius, and apparently defeated by him in battle, are referred to by the Roman panegyrist Eumenius as *Picti*, the Picts. This, in 297, is the first mention of the name, though it refers to the Picts as well-known enemies of the Britons. Another praise poem, a few years later, refers to the woods and marshes of the 'Caledonians, Picts and others'. The name is clearly intended as a generic one, rather than that of one tribe.

Most older books on the Picts state bluntly that the name means 'painted people', since the Latin name *Picti* is the plural form of *pictus*, meaning 'painted'. Some writers are more cautious: 'derived from the Picts' own name for themselves, or possibly a Latin nickname meaning "the painted ones'"(Foster, 11). There is no evidence at all that it was the Picts' name for themselves, or even that, in the third century, they had any generic name for themselves. Eumenius uses it in a way that suggests it had already been current for some time. Before that, Ptolemy around 150 had identified a number of tribes north and west of the Forth-Clyde line, including the Caledones; and Tacitus, in the late first century, had used Caledones as an umbrella name for all the northern tribes. At the time of Theodosius's campaigns in 365, the Picts were reported as divided into two groups, the Dicaledones and the Verturiones. This is the last historical mention of the Caledones; W. J. Watson suggests the Di- prefix means that they were in two divisions, separated by the Mounth. The Verturiones gave their name to the Pictish province or kingdom of Fortriu. As there were no recorded migrations into the region (apart from that of the Scots), all these names must refer to the same people, or group of peoples. By the time of Gildas, in the mid-sixth century, the name of Picts appears to be the accepted one for inhabitants of northern Scotland. W. J. Watson, the most erudite philologist to examine the word 'Pict', concluded from examination of similar forms in other languages that it is a native word, *Pect* in its original form; and he relates it to the Pictones, a Gaulish tribe from the Biscay coast. He rejects the Latin *pictus* origin, pointing out that as all the ancient inhabitants of Britain apparently dyed themselves, 'the term is not a differentia' (*Proceedings of the Gaelic Society of Inverness*, XXX,1921). (He does not apply this argument to the Smertae, however, whom he takes to be the 'Smeared Folk'). As with other Pictish origins, the meaning of the Picts' name seems untraceable.

At least into the first two centuries, it is possible that the people of the far north were not all of Celtic speech, but preserved a language spoken there since before the Bronze Age. A. P. Smyth, in his history of early Scotland,*Warlords and Holy Men*, attacks this notion of a pre-Celtic language in the far

north. He convincingly establishes that a Celtic-speaking aristocracy was in control there as elsewhere. But he does not pursue what he admits to be evidence of 'diverse cultural streams
among the Picts which may well have political implications'.
Even if there are no significant political implications, there is
evidence of cultural diversity both between the Picts as a group
and the Scots and Britons, and within the Pictish territory
itself. The question as to whether the Picts had certain unique
attributes or traditions, including language, remains open. It is
worth repeating, with Dr Smyth, that there are no grounds for
regarding the Picts as a single people. The name is best kept as
a general one that refers to all the inhabitants of the country
north of and beyond the Antonine Wall (i.e. including Arran
and Kintyre), prior to the arrival of Scots colonists from
Ireland. They may have comprised several different peoples.

Dr Watson came to the view that the change of name from
Caledones to Picts meant a political change, signalling a dominance by northerners after the fourth century:

'While the hegemony of the tribes was held by the
Caledonians, the tribes were styled collectively Caledonians
and their country was known as Caledonia; when the hegemony passed to the Picts, the tribes formerly called
Caledonians were called collectively Picts, and their country
. . . came to be called in Latin, Pictavia. At a still later date,
and for exactly the same reason, came the further change to
Scots and Scotia.'

Watson believed that in these societies the Celts were the 'ruling race': a military aristocracy self-imposed over the 'pre-
Celtic people, forming doubtless the bulk of the population,
and themselves of more than one racial origin'. Most modern
scholars doubt this 'invasion' theory.

These were the peoples whom Contantius invaded in 306. It
was his second military campaign in the British island, but his

first in Caledonia. The old Roman fort at Carpow was reacti-
vated, as was the fleet's depot at Cramond. It seems likely that
Constantius followed very much the same route as Severus had
100 years before. As with Severus's invasion, the inhabitants
repaired their defences or created new ones; in the northeast,
renewed fortifications at Portsoy and at Burghead appear to
date from around 300. Scotland being the northernmost territory that Roman emperors and their entourages reached in person, there was a keen interest among Constantius's court, as
there had been in Severus's, on such phenomena as the long
light northern summer evenings – they had a real sense of
reaching to the outer limits of the world they ruled.

Like Severus, Constantius was a sick man, and he too died
on his return to York. His son Constantine, who had been with
him on the invasion, was immediately acclaimed Augustus by
the troops. Like Severus's sons, his attention was then focused
on his need to impose his hold upon the continental empire.
Whether or not this was the reason, the Constantian expedition did not succeed in pushing the empire's boundaries
beyond their existing limits. But the north was not unscathed.
Again like Severus's, Constantius's invasion appears to have
been one of destruction and terror tactics, and wrought
enough damage to keep the Picts from mounting any serious
offensive for three decades. After the 'Verona List' of 313,
which refers to 'Picts and Caledonians', it is 342 before they
are mentioned again by a Roman chronicler. Constantine may
have been more active in the aggression against them than his
ailing father Constantius, or perhaps it was his later fame as
'Constantine the Great', the first Christian emperor, that
impressed the Picts enough to adopt a version of his name for
some of their later kings.

Meanwhile, Hadrian's Wall was once again the frontier line.
At some point, probably between 315 and 318, Constantine as
emperor assumed the title of Britannicus Maximus, suggesting that all had not been peace among either the Brigantes or

the Maeatae, and that his generals had won an important battle, but no details are known.

Much of the fourth century was relatively peaceful for the provinces of Britannia. Some time before 314, they were reorganised into a set of four, collectively known as the *vicarius Britanniarum*, vicarate of the Britains, and forming part of a larger grouping, the Prefecture of the Gauls, with its headquarters at Trier. By this time, here and there, small Christian communities had formed, led by soldiers or merchants converted in Italy, Syria, or Gaul, and who had brought their new beliefs with them. From 313, it had been legal to practise their religion within the empire. Tiny pockets within an overwhelmingly pagan context, they however were inspired to spread their faith with a sense of mission that paganism did not possess. But the focus of empire was now shifting far eastwards with the transformation of Byzantium, on the Bosporus, into Constantinople, 'new Rome'. The provinces of Britannia, on the western edge of the western half of the empire, an island on three sides and with a hostile border on the fourth, began to appear vulnerable. The Picts had been temporarily subdued rather than pacified. The inhabitants of Ireland, the Hiberni, also called the Scoti after Scota, their legendary ancestress, were increasingly ready to raid across the Irish Sea. And, on the far side of the North Sea, beyond the northern edge of the empire, barbarian tribes, Angles, Jutes, and Saxons, speakers of Indo-Germanic languages and with their own set of pagan gods, were massing.

Constantine died in 337, and a struggle for supremacy broke out among his sons. Probably as a result, the Picts were back in hostile action in 342, in what may have been concerted campaigns with the Scots, raiding through the Southern Uplands – still an area of Roman influence and patrolled by Roman troops. These raids were on a large enough scale to bring Constans, now western emperor, to the frontier in person, in a wintertime visit intended to accomplish strategic reorganisation of the area north of Hadrian's Wall. A future emperor, Gratian, was appointed as a military count to restore order. Terms were made with the Picts, perhaps involving subsidies. Currency remained unused north of the Wall, but gold in coin or ingot form was always welcome to kings and chiefs. They made use of it in their own gift-exchanging, but also in the making of jewellery and in other decorative arts.

The empire's own troubles were to provide more opportunities for attacks. Constans was killed, and the position of western co-emperor was seized by the soldier Magnentius, who again took much of the army away from Britain to support his claim. Although he was defeated by Constantius II, in a battle far away in Pannonia in 351, his rule survived until 353.

Seven years later, with the western empire newly under the rule of the Caesar Julian, the Picts combined with the Scots to repeat the raids of 342, and though the arrival of Lupicinus, Julian's *magister militum* (army commander) with reinforcements, put a stop to the campaign, the raids resumed after his departure. Clearly the provinces of Britannia, by this time under the rule of civilian governors, no longer had a sufficient standing army to protect them, and raiding from the north continued intermittently into the 360s. In 365, the scale of the incursions increased and, two years later, the barbarians seemed likely to overrun the whole Roman domain. The Roman writer, Ammianus Marcellinus, refers at this time to a *barbarica conspiratio*, concerted action by Picts, Scots, and Saxons; also with another northern tribe or confederation called the Attacotti, who are not otherwise recorded. It has been assumed that they came from the Western Isles, but their fleeting appearance serves as a reminder of the gaps that exist in our knowledge of the composition and locations of the tribal groups.

By 367, the raiding reached a peak. The two most senior Roman commanders were killed or captured and Britannia was reduced to a state bordering on anarchy. The collusion of the invading tribes did not, however, mean that they were aiming at a formal conquest. To them, Britannia appears to have been simply a great storehouse of plunderable goods, from which in due course they returned home with their booty. For the Romano-British, this offered the unpleasant prospect of repairing their homes and temples, and replanting their crops, only to face more attacks by tattooed raiders in the following year.

The troubles in Britain coincided with difficulties for the empire on other frontiers, and the depleted and demoralised army put up little resistance. The Pictish raiders were now reaching as far south as the Romano-British capital, London. Then, in early 368, they found themselves faced by a Roman general as able, ruthless, and active as any governor from the previous centuries. This was the Spanish-born military count Theodosius (accompanied by his son, the future emperor Theodosius), sent with four regiments by the emperor Valentinian to restore order. How far north Theodosius penetrated is unclear; a praise poem by Claudian, written some time later, claims that he camped 'amid the snows of Caledonia' and that his ships reached Orkney and Thule (Shetland), defeating Saxons and Picts respectively, but the whole work is pitched in generalised and conventional terms with no verifying details. Undoubtedly, however, the raiders were forced out of the south, the shattered systems of provincial administration and army deployment were put back in place, and a new fifth province, Valentia, was set up. This region may have been in the northwest, around Carlisle: a Romano-British district deliberately created to block a main point of entry from the north.

The northerners also once again found Hadrian's Wall restored and regarrisoned. Many of them were pressed or bought into Roman service, as auxiliary troops. Four Attacotti regiments are recorded. It also seems likely that Theodosius abolished the *areani*, who may have become disaffected, allying themselves with the hostile tribes. Instead of a force of spies and hill patrols, the Roman administration established the Votadini and perhaps also the Damnonii as formal allies of the empire,

client statelets with Latin titles for their kings. The former tribe
had been friendly neighbours to the Romano-Britons for centuries by this time. Their leader Padarn (Latin *Paternus*) was
recorded as Padarn Pesrut, 'Padarn of the red cloak: a symbol of
imperial authority' (Frere, 341). The Damnonii lands were to
become the core territory of the kingdom of Strathclyde, and
the genealogy of the later kings of Strathclyde shows two rulers
with Latin names, from the later fourth century.

The rise of a coordinated Pictish kingdom to the north was
a serious threat to those southern tribes, making it more likely
that they would strengthen their alliances with the empire.
And also with each other: in the course of the fifth century, the
Damnonii and Novantae, perhaps with other tribes including
all or some of the Selgovae, united together in the Cumbric-
speaking kingdom of Strathclyde, whose capital, Alclut – the
rock of Clyde – was on Dumbarton Rock. Pressed into, and
paid for, an alliance with the revitalised administration of
Britannia, the southern tribes assumed a formal status of hostility to the Caledonians. The Picts responded in part by taking
to the sea, their fleets bypassing the guarded frontier and join-
ing with the Scots in attacking vulnerable coastal areas further
south. The troubles of the western empire thus played an
important part in the formation of the power blocs beyond its
frontier. These would live on after the empire's end; the hostility between the friends of Rome and the barbarians of the
north continued in the relations between the kingdoms of
Strathclyde and Pictland, which were rarely cordial.

The End of Empire

The empire was in increasing disarray. The reinstated Wall and
new coastal defences and signal stations set up by Theodosius
in 370 preserved the integrity of the Roman provinces for little
more than a generation. In 383, a Roman general commanding
in Britannia, the Spanish-born Magnus Maximus, rebelled

against the rule of the emperor Gratian. Five years later, he was defeated and killed in battle against the emperor Theodosius I. Magnus's campaigns were fought in Gaul, and many troops were again withdrawn from Britain to support him. During Magnus's period in power, the Picts and Scots invaded the provinces of Britannia but he defeated them, apparently returning from Gaul in 384 to do so. Magnus's memory was preserved in Galloway (as it also was in Wales) as the founder of a dynasty of rulers; it is likely that he drew the Novantae or another large tribal group into alliance in his short and successful campaign against the Picts, and quite possible that a daughter or daughters of his married tribal kings. But after Magnus's demise, raiding from the north and west resumed.

It was not until the very end of the century that the empire again responded; and for the last time. Under the orders, and perhaps the actual command, of the Vandal general Stilicho, who was in effective charge of the western empire under its young ruler Honorius, a punitive expedition was sent by land and sea; writing around 400, Honorius's court poet Claudian tells of Stilicho making the sea foam with hostile oars. Once again the Picts were pushed back and, by 399, Stilicho was able to claim that the security of the British provinces had been restored. But on the continent he had the vast incursions of the Goths under Alaric to withstand. Troops were yet again withdrawn from Britain to fight elsewhere, an event that must have been despairingly familiar to the Romano-British provincials. These were not only Roman legions, but perhaps largely auxiliary forces, including regiments raised from tribes beyond the frontier, such as the Attacotti. If the Votadini and other border tribes were also made to contribute, this would have further reduced their fighting strength against their implacable northern and western neighbours.

The western empire was fighting for its life. The residual troops left in Britannia, aware that they could not cope with the raids to come, were mutinous and raised a succession of their own chosen leaders as 'emperors' of the embattled provinces. Their domain sometimes included Gaul and even Spain; there were three between 406 and 411, when the last of them, who had taken the name Constantine, was defeated by Honorius in Gaul. But Honorius's resources could not stretch to re-establishing control of Britannia. By 410, there were virtually no Roman soldiers still under effective discipline in the island. Even before Constantine's defeat, the provincials had taken their government and defence into their own hands. The chronicler Zosimus wrote, with his mind chiefly on the situation in Gaul:

'The barbarians across the Rhine attacked everywhere with all their power, and brought the inhabitants of Britain and some of the nations of Gaul to the point of revolting from Roman rule and living on their own, no longer obedient to Roman laws. The Britons took up arms and, braving danger for their own independence, freed their cities from the barbarians threatening them . . . expelling their Roman governors and establishing their own administration as best they could.'

The barbarians mentioned by Zosimus may have included invaders from across the North Sea, as well as those from within the British Isles. It is notable that he attributes success to the home-guard operations mounted by the Romano-Britons. Many communities had built walls around themselves in the third and fourth centuries, and there may have been a withdrawal into these fortified towns, leaving the countryside, with its many rich villa-farms, open to the ravagers. The emperor Honorius himself acknowledged the reality of the position in a letter to a section of the Romano-British community which had apparently appealed to him for help – he told them they must look after their own defence. This was not a formal abandonment; a resurgent empire would surely have re-established its control over the wealthy provinces of Britannia. But Rome's western empire never recovered.

From the Picts' point of view, the situation must have appeared promising, but not without problems. Even though they had long been circumventing the southern tribes, and Hadrian's Wall, by seaborne attacks down both coasts, they now knew the Wall had no garrison and there was no early likelihood of a garrison returning. There was no backup of armoured legions to sustain the Votadini and the other frontier tribes. On the other hand, these were no longer cut off from their natural allies south of the Wall. In combination with the Brigantes, they would provide formidable opposition to any raiding force from the north. The Picts also found that, as Zosimus reports, the Romano-British communities did not crumble into anarchy: left to themselves, they began to organise and fight back, providing more serious resistance than the Picts had met since Stilicho's intervention a decade before.

The first known British war leader is Vortigern, a Celtic title rather than a personal name, meaning 'great lord', who established his rule in 425. Vortigern is credited, or blamed, with having brought in the Angles and Saxons as allies against the Picts and Scots, thus leading to the eventual overthrow of the Brittonic kingdoms and the establishment of the Anglo-Saxon-Danish kingdom of England. Another figure, the bishop Germanus from Gaul, is also recorded as leading a British army against a combined force of Picts and Saxons, and defeating them, possibly in North Wales, in 429. Prior to this victory, Germanus – formerly a Roman general – had conducted a mass baptism of his army and, in legend, it is known as the 'Alelluia Victory', after the Christians' war cry. The religious aspect of this victory may have been played up after the event; but it could have impressed the Picts with the warlike attributes of the Christian deity.

A similar legend is attached to one of their own later battles, at Athelstaneford. In the mid- and later fifth century, the dim figures of Ambrosius and the even hazier Arthur appear as leaders of the Britons' resistance to barbarian incursion. Although

Vortigern perceived the Picts as the main danger, the later invasions of the Germanic tribes were by far the most systematic,
steady and decisive. The Picts appear to have maintained their
traditional seasonal pattern of raids and retirals. The others were
coming to stay. Pressure was also maintained from the west.
From early in the fifth century, forces of the high king 'Niall of
the Nine Hostages', the Scots (i.e. Irish), had been raiding
fiercely up the Bristol Channel and on the Welsh coast, and
determined attempts were made to found colonies. Wales might
ultimately have become a 'Scotland' but for the movement, perhaps at the instigation of Vortigern or another British high king,
of the British tribal leader, Cunedda (grandson of Padarn
Pesrut), and his people from Manau Gododdin, the kingdom of
the Votadini, to the northern part of Wales. This may have
occurred in the 440s. Modern historians tend to disallow the
Cunedda story, which has no objective proof, and is first
recorded by the ninth-century British writer, Nennius, in his
Historia Brittonum, which retails many a fable. But some action
effectively repressed further attempts at the colonisation of
Gwynedd from the west. If the migration did occur, its scale
does not appear to have greatly weakened the Votadini.

New and Old Religions

In other ways as well as Germanus's divinely aided militancy,
the Christian church was an important element in sustaining
the Romano-British communities. From its beginnings in isolated groups of scattered worshippers, the Christian religion
had made great advances during the later third and early fourth
centuries. There was a tenuous structure of British bishoprics.
Many of the population still remained pagan or semipagan but,
for others, there was a faith to defend against the barbarians, as
well as a way of life to be valued. Christianity was also established north of the Wall in the favourable territory of the
Novantae. Around 397, St Ninian, returned from a theological

education in Rome and perhaps also under St Martin at Tours, founded or joined the church, Candida Casa, at Whithorn. It was a bridgehead, a little mission station like those that 19th-century Scottish missionaries would set up in Africa.

The missionaries were bringing their new faith to bear against an ancient structure of beliefs, myths, and rituals, accreted over centuries, and firmly embedded in the social life of the people. Fertility, origins, death, and the causes of natural events are the basic subject matter of early religion.

There is ample evidence on the ground in Scotland that early inhabitants, from the latter part of the Stone Age and into the Bronze Age, were very much preoccupied by death. Their grave monuments, houses of the dead, were much larger and more imposing than the houses of the living. Enormous energy and thousands of man-hours went into the making of these funeral sites. What beliefs they represent about life beyond the grave can only be guessed at. But by the early centuries CE, whether or not beliefs had changed, the business of burial had become far less of a massive undertaking. Most Pictish burial sites consist of long cists, shallow, rectangular graves lined with stone slabs, suggesting that bodies were buried rather than cremated. Some of the cist burials are grouped and covered by an earth platform to form a low barrow, and often Pictish symbol stones have been found in association with these. These unelaborate graves suggest a more matter-of-fact view of death, but there may be other explanations of which we know nothing.

Rather more is known about the relationship of religious belief and natural events, though the information is virtually all from continental and Irish sources rather than Pictish ones. Before the conversion of the Celtic peoples to Christianity, their kings had a dual role, as war leaders and as prime figures in the religious life of their people. The evidence for this is extensive, though almost entirely from sources and commentaries relating to the tribes of Gaul and of Roman Britain, and to the Gaels of

Ireland. While it may reasonably be supposed that the functions of British (Strathclyde) and Pictish kings were similar, it may equally well be supposed that there were significant differences. By the first century CE, in Celtic and other societies, an elaborate system of mediation between people and nature had evolved. Among the Celtic tribes, this system was maintained and applied by a particular order of society, the druids. They were a high-status group recruited from among the noble families. In some cases, a king might himself be a druid, which implies that he had gone through the 20-year training required to make a young man or woman proficient in the knowledge and skills of the order. Even without this exceptional preparation, a member of a king's *derbfine*, or kindred group, would be likely to know what was required of a king when he participated in the rites of the druids' oak grove, or in casting offerings to a sacred pool or stream, or in examining omens and auspices.

Most of what information there is on the druids' cults is given by foreign reporters, perhaps hostile witnesses. But the prevalence of human sacrifice in the first two centuries CE, if not later, is plain:

> 'Their predilection for human sacrifice is incontestable, and the descriptions of the great wicker-work images which were filled with men and animals and then set on fire is reminiscent of the descriptions in the early Irish tales of the trapping of heroes in the *bruidne*, the so-called hostelries, and the subsequent burning of these.' (Anne Ross, *Pagan Celtic Britain*)

Dr Nora Chadwick suggests that such holocausts were rare, and probably related to times of extreme tension (*The Celts*). The first-century Roman poet Lucan made his readers' flesh creep with descriptions of the reeking altars and bloody groves of the druids, where bodies and parts of bodies hung in trees as propitiation to savage deities. His contemporary, Pliny, referred to Britain as: 'spellbound by magic and conducts so much ritual that it would seem that it was Britain that had given magic to the Persians' (*Natural History*, 30.13). The Romans never sought to understand the basis of Celtic beliefs, and could see the Celtic gods only in relation to their own Graeco-Roman pantheon.

By the later fifth century, it is likely that human sacrifice was very little practised by the Caledonians or the Scots. Such things would have been even more abhorrent to Christians than were other heathen practices, but though Columba remonstrated – to little avail – against such still-current pagan notions as the universal habit of looking for omens in everything, none of the early saints seems to have had cause to fulminate against druidic sacrifices. How far there was still a cultic significance in the decapitation of bodies is unclear. Christianity did not put a stop to this, any more than it did to warfare in general. The Celtic tribes were head-hunters and, while this may bring the word 'barbarian' back in a rush, it does not seem that lopping off heads was an nondiscriminating activity. The desired heads were those of enemies defeated in battle, which were exhibited at the victorious warrior's door, and also – before Christianity – in the druidic sanctuary.

By the fourth century, in the time of the first missionary saints, there was a vast body of druidical learning and lore; and although references are made to druids' books, it seems most likely that the great bulk of this was taught by rote and committed to memory, in the same way that the Indian Vedic hymns were preserved (with great accuracy) for centuries. The wider organisation of the druids is not known. In the first and second centuries, the island of Môn (Anglesey) had been the centre of the druidic cult of the British and perhaps also of the Gaulish tribes, but this role had been smashed by the Romans in 60CE. There is nothing to suggest that there was an archdruid in later times and, if the way in which the Christian Church was organised is a guide, then each provincial kingdom, with its group of *tuatha*, would have had its own druids, members of its own

leading families. Druids had the right to move between kingdoms, as did bards, and thus had opportunities to confer; and no
doubt often acted as ambassadors or emissaries (see below). The
profound conservatism built into the system by their training
process was a guard against innovation or heresy, though it is
very unlikely that heresy was a concept of theirs. It was not a
cult that demanded fervent faith or abstract love, or that set a
moral code. The notions of sin and retribution seem scarcely to
have been present. Despite the placing of the hero-champion at
the peak of achievement, they were not individualists; this is
seen in their law codes, where the tribe or kindred always took
responsibility for a single member's action. Such a collective
spirit does not accord well with the doctrine of personal salva-
tion, and helps to explain why the Gaels had difficulty in accepting the notion of hell. Julius Caesar was of the opinion that the
Gauls believed in the transmigration of souls. But their cult had
a supreme preoccupation with fertility and a keen sense of the
living earth. This was not in the Gaian or superecological sense
of today, but in terms of natural features being animated by spirits, which lived as the stream or field itself but could also have an
identity given to them, often that of an animal. So certain
streams might be 'bull streams', certain lochs 'horse lochs'.
These identities remain fossilised in such names as the River
Tarff ('bull') or Loch Eck ('horse'). Tribute was paid to these
watery spirits of place by casting precious objects into the water.
In fact, just as animal sacrificers, though offering the beast to the
god, usually ate the meat and left the bones for the deity, many
of the more routine offerings may have been weapons and uten-
sils somewhat past their best. Often they were broken, though
the breaking may have been part of the ritual.

More than 400 names of deities worshipped by the Celtic
peoples of Europe and the British Isles have been identified,
most of them, as Dr Nora Chadwick points out, found only
once (*The Celts*), and even recurrent names tend to be restricted
to a particular region. Not one of these names comes from

Scotland. In Romanised Gaul and south Britain, many names were carved in stone at sacred sites; in Ireland, many names have been preserved in the oral tradition that was ultimately written down. North of Hadrian's Wall, where writing seems to have been unknown or very rare until the fifth century, there are no inscriptions. Our ignorance of Pictish mythology leaves only the Pictish carved stones, certain place names, and archaeological finds to offer clues to the gods and goddesses of the Picts. It is reasonable to suppose that their cult shared the general characteristics of that of their southern neighbours. Within the same overall seasonal pattern that determined most of their forms of ritual, it seems that many tribes had their own specific deities. On the other hand, the broad types of god, goddess, or spirit seem to have shared many similarities among the peoples, as Dr Anne Ross demonstrates in the pages of *Pagan Celtic Britain*, and some of these resemblances remained constant over considerable periods of time.

Some scanty evidence is found in place names. Most identifiably Pictish place names refer to landscape features and to land divisions. But a number of river names, such as Dee and Don (both indicative of a divinity) and Nethy (indicative of purity) suggest a cult connection. In a fascinating argument in *The Picts and Their Place Names*, Dr Bill Nicolaisen looks at reasons for supposing that Aber- names may indicate something more than a river mouth or confluence, perhaps denoting the cultic significance of such a place. The names of Arbuthnot, which preserves both aber- and a river name which notes healing qualities, and Aberfeldy, which preserves that of a *pellaidh*, or water spirit, show connections with the supernatural. Some of the -tarff ('bull') place names are also Pictish in origin. Nearly all these are water names, showing that the Picts found the same inspiration in water sites as did the Brigantians and other tribes of Britain and Gaul.

The archaeological evidence is even scantier. The discovery of a collection of bull carvings at and near the Pictish coastal fort at Burghead has led to speculation of a bull cult there. Although Anne Ross has traced elements of preservation, in a much-attenuated form, of the head cult and of the protective local deity, into the 20th-century society of the Highlands (*The Druids*), Scotland in general has been a much less fruitful source of pagan Celtic cult objects than south Britain and continental Europe; and much of the Caledonians' and other tribes' religious practice can only be inferred. Of course, many cult objects would have been carved out of wood, with a much lower chance of survival, though one or two striking wooden items have been found from pre-Pictish times, like the five-foot high female idol figure found near Ballachulish and dated to the early centuries CE.

The tribes who lived north of Cheviot around the time of Christ dwelt, as we still do, among the monuments of ancient predecessors. But, without the vastly greater population, the tamed countryside, and the residential sprawl of today, these monuments were far more apparent. While this was especially true for Orcadians and the inhabitants of west Lewis, who had Brogar, Stenness, and Callanish (not yet enveloped in the rising peat) to gaze at, there were hundreds of stone circles throughout the country, often close to imposing burial mounds. Whatever their original purpose, it is likely that some of these were adapted to forms of worship presided over by the druids, even if it was only by providing a sacred site. Since modern research has tended to dismiss the notion of 'invasions' of new populations in the pre-Christian eras, with all that that implies in the way of cultural shocks and drastic changes in customs, in favour of a far more gradual process, it would seem likely that the stone circles were at no time regarded as alien constructions but as a 'heritage', part of the living tradition, even if the original purpose was lost. Many generations on, a tall stone with Bronze-Age cup marks on its base would be used in the eighth century as a Christian cross slab (Meigle No. 1).

The Saints Come In

Faced with this great hedge of cultic beliefs, superstitions, and practices, the Christian pioneers had one or two important weapons. The chief one was their religion's in-built urge to evangelise, to make others believe the gospel news with the same intensity as themselves. Such a drive was foreign to the druidic cult, which was formed out of customary procedures, and which, shared by the whole population, had no need to proselytise. For the same reason, it had had no cause to defend itself. It had never been attacked before and its passivity made it vulnerable, like some lumbering herbivore suddenly confronted by a new and sharp-toothed species. Vastly outnumbered as they were, the missionaries knew that other populations had been won over; moreover, since the time of Constantine the Great, the Roman Empire had officially adopted Christianity (apart from the brief reign of Julian). Though collapsed in the west, the empire was still mighty in the east. This may or may not have helped the cause, but the prestige it brought was undeniable. The Latin liturgy and the communion ceremony were rich in mystique. Christianity could not be ignored.

In another respect, the missionaries had an advantage over the druids. Ironically, they were the inheritors of much classical pagan knowledge and educational technique, passed on by and learned from the Greeks, whose colony-towns could be found from Marseilles to the Black Sea. They had some understanding of the art of rhetoric, of disputation and the presentation of argument. The druids had no such linguistic structures to defend their position. But intellectual arguments rarely win converts and, in the one recorded confrontation of saint and druid, between Columcille and Broichan, it is the saint's superior magic, not his debating skill, that wins the day. Miracles are ascribed to most of the Celtic saints, and they played important roles as averters of evil. Perhaps because he had been a figure hitherto missing from people's lives, the saints took to the devil in a strong way. St Serf had a conversation with him in a cave on the Fife coast. Even on the holy isle of Iona, St Columba had to take precautions against an evil spirit lodged in a milk pail. But, at that time, the spirits and the icons of paganism were still very much present, deeply lodged in popular belief and imagination. Centuries later, some of them would still figure in Pictish stone carving, like the horned Cernunnos figure at Meigle.

Still, the religion of peace, of humility, of 'love thy neighbour' and 'turn the other cheek', of renunciation of worldly things, of original sin and the need for atonement, cannot have been easy to incorporate into a society founded on a basis of rank, conspicuous display, slavery, and armed raiding. The Picts and Scots, however, saw things from their own standpoint. In the fourth century, at the 'Alleluia Battle', the Picts had a chance to note the efficacy of the Christian God as a war leader, and the Old Testament supplied further evidence of this. Asceticism and the monastic life clearly had appeal to many of the Gaels, sometimes in forms of the most austere and solitary sort, as in the beehive huts of Hebridean isles and islets, as far away as North Rona. Eventually, with the conversion, through the seventh and eighth centuries, of the Anglo-Saxons and of the Franks, Christianity and the Latin language would be of practical value in providing links and conduits, enabling contact with other peoples and kingdoms. But this had nothing to do with the original acceptance of the new religion.

Very little is known for sure about the bringers of Christianity to the Picts and Britons. More is known about St Patrick, who went from Britain to Ireland, than about those who made the journey in the other direction after his death (with the great exception of St Columba). Marjorie Anderson remarked that 'there is hardly an Irish saint associated with Scotland in the sixth century for whom the evidence is more than barely admissible'. Even with St Ninian, despite his reputation, there is no real evidence as to his life span, his education, and his achievements. St Kentigern's origin, though furnished with many accurate local details, is a legendary tale. The details and impressions that we have of men like these come from life stories written in their praise centuries later and. though they may incorporate authentic details from manuscripts now lost, there is no way of telling. The sainthood of Celtic clerics was neither awarded nor confirmed by the Bishop of Rome in his Lateran Palace. It was the verdict of their contemporaries and followers. Their familiar names suggest a sort of proprietorial affection among the people for some of these pioneers. Grand Kentigern, founder of the Church at Glasgow, whose name means 'great lord', was also known as Mungo meaning 'dear one'. St Luoc, St Laise, and others had the qualifier *mo-* placed in front of their personal names, with the sense of 'dear' or 'dear little', still preserved in place names like Kilmoluag and Lamlash.

Whatever the true facts of Ninian's story may be, archaeology has confirmed the existence of an ancient church at the site of Ninian's **Candida Casa** or 'white house', at Whithorn (which itself is from the Anglian words meaning 'white house') and other Christian sites, from around 500CE. Christianity was established in this area soon after, or perhaps even before, the Romans left, though only in isolated pockets. Its first practitioners may have been simply Christian merchants or farmers, rather than missionary evangelists. From such nuclei the new faith spread among the Britons, though the twelfth-century *Life of Kentigern* by Jocelyn of Furness says that their first Christian king, Rhyderch, in the late sixth century, was baptised in Ireland and that he subsequently summoned Kentigern (who was of the Gododdin rather than the Strathclyde Britons) from Wales, to where he had removed himself. In his study, *Medieval Wales*, David Walker points out that:

'All this could be legend, rather than fact . . . No ancient dedication has been claimed for him.'

A number of writers have noted that it is curious that Ninian, with his base in the extreme southwest, should be associated chiefly with missionary work up the east coast – although he, as, apparently, a bishop not an abbot, was not tied down to any one monastery, and Jocelyn also notes that Ninian had formed a Christian community in Glasgow, long before Kentigern. Despite the many St Ninian dedications, Dr Kathleen Hughes noted:

> 'There is no early evidence to show that the commemora-
> tions to Ninian in Pictland are early, and since the form of
> his name in such commemorations is either latinised or in
> a Gaelic form derived through Scots vernacular the com-
> memorations may go back only to a later development of his
> cult' (Hughes, 49).

That could mean the twelfth century, when Aelred's *Life of Ninian* was written and interest in the saint was clearly high.

How widely and deeply Christianity spread among the ordinary people is impossible to say. The Celtic Church, in its Pictish, British, and Scottish forms, may not have been a reli-gion of the 'masses', but may, like the druidic cult that pre-ceded it, rather have been essentially the preserve of the upper ranks. The number of churches specifically mentioned in Pictland during the time of the Pictish kingdoms is small. The churches themselves were generally built of wood, or wattle and daub, and were very small. Their purpose was for monks and priests to sing their offices and celebrate the Mass for themselves and perhaps a few privileged lay people. Preaching was an activity for outdoors. It is most likely to have been at a temporary outside altar that the common people were given communion, perhaps on an infrequent basis, coinciding with church festivals and local saints' days.

Perhaps in continuity with the Druidic cult, the church in each tribal area was ruled not by a bishop but by an abbot.

He was normally a member of a royal family and thus very much involved in the maintaining of that royal line and in the family's administration of its kingdom. Late in the Pictish kingdom, an abbot might not be a cleric at all, like Crinan, the layman who bore the title abbot of Dunkeld, and who married the daughter of king Malcolm II and was father of king Duncan. Less is known about Celtic abbesses, but they too could be persons of note, like Darlugdach, abbess of Kildare, who is noted in the Pictish king list as having come to the founding of St Brigid's Church at Abernethy in the time of king Nectan macMorbet, around the end of the sixth century. In the role of the abbots lay an important difference betweeen the Celtic Churches and the Church as ruled from Rome. In the Roman scheme of things, the bishop was of prime importance; in the Celtic Churches the bishop had no territorial authority, no authority to impose doctrine, and very little judicial or disciplinary power. His role was a sacramental one, in the anointing of priests, and in this way an apostolic link with St Peter was kept up. Bishops were greatly respected, but strictly as holy men. Power lay with the abbots.

CHAPTER THREE

Dàl Riada

Early Colonists

As we have seen, during the fourth and fifth centuries, the Picts and the Scots had no cause to quarrel with each other. The treasure house of Britannia offered quite enough in the way of battle and booty to keep both sets of peoples fully occupied. Indeed, from the fourth century on, they appear often to have acted in concert. Neither people had much to covet from the other, with one important exception. Ireland, with its wide plains, its more temperate climate, and its gold, was richer and more populous than Pictland. It had not suffered invasion since a far-off legendary past, and even those invaders were seen as the ancestors of its present ruling elements. The Picts, on the other hand, had been savaged at recurrent intervals by punitive Roman expeditions. Even though much of their territory, in the north and west, had never been reached by Roman troops, the repeated route taken by Roman armies suggests that their main centres were to the east and north of the Mounth, from Strathmore to Buchan and Moray. Much manpower had been lost through slaughter, enslavement, and perhaps conscription into the imperial forces (though no specifically Pictish units are recorded). Ptolemy, around 150CE, assigns several tribal names to the western mainland between Kintyre and Cape Wrath. He assigns none to the Hebrides, though this need not mean there were no tribes there. The islands were well populated in pre-history and, around the year 250, seem to have been a separate subkingdom. The third-century Roman writer and 'collector of memorable things', Julius Solinus, records from an unknown source of information that:

> 'The isles of the Hebudae are ... governed by one King. This monarch has no property. He is supported at the public expense ... lest he should be tempted by avarice to commit any acts of oppression, poverty confines him within the rules of justice. He has no personal interest to promote. He has no wife, that can with any propriety be called his own.'

But, quite early in the British Christian Era, the Hebrides were noted as empty, and inhabited only by spirits. This 'desert' aspect was at the centre of their appeal to monks and holy hermits. Even though Pictland had a much greater proportion of inhospitable ground above the 500m (1500ft) contour than Ireland, there were many areas suitable for local habitation. In Ireland, by contrast, there was a degree of land hunger in the late fifth century, caused by the combination of population growth and intertribal conflict, in which leading families, with their followers, were forced out of territorial holdings.

According to later sources, a highly significant migration took place at the end of the fifth century. A people known as the Dàl Riata, from northeast Ulster, moved the short distance to Kintyre, Lorn, and the adjacent islands. Its leader was Fergus MacErc, and he was accompanied by two brothers, Loarn and Oengus. The arrival of this princely family may have been to consolidate the rule of what was already a substantial, if scattered, collection of colonies, and the effect was to transfer the Dàl Riatan tribal kingship to the new colony, from where its Irish territory was also governed. The legendary story of the beginnings of the Dàl Riada colony may represent the formalisation of its existence as a kingdom, around the year 500. At this time, the centre, or main centre, of Pictish rule was in the north, at Inverness. The allegiance of the colonists was not to the Pictish king, Drest, but continued to be given to the overking of Ulster. Drest appears to have tolerated the colony's existence. The reasons for his accommodating attitude to the Scots are unknown. Although the Argyll colony was not a modest affair, the wealth and strength of Ulster may have been enough to make the Pictish king and his advisers feel it was best to acquiesce in a state of affairs they would not have initiated. Possibly the part of their domain soon to be called Argyll ('coastland of the Gael') seemed of little strategic concern. H. M. Chadwick suggested that a part was played by 'British or Welsh diplomacy', since the colony formed a buffer zone between Strathclyde and the Picts:

> 'The result of the foundation of the Irish kingdom of Dalriada was to render the Welsh of southern Scotland practically immune from Pictish attacks.'

While this is possible, it remains a speculation. In those times, any neighbour was likely to prove troublesome sooner or later, and the benefit to the Picts of any such deal is not apparent.

Origins

One of the problems in giving an accurate account of events in this era is that all the documentary information comes from much later, and is either 'Scottish', written in Gaelic by scribes predisposed to present a view of events favourable to the incoming Scots, or 'British', equally concerned to promote the position of the kingdom of Strathclyde. With the exception of their stone carvings and a few linguistic hints, what we know of the Picts comes from the comments of others, first Romans, then Gaels and Britons, all with their own perspective on the northerners. Partisans deeply engaged in the political and moral debates of their own times, they had no use for objective historical accounts, as we understand the notion. History had to be shaped to underwrite the present and the hoped-for future, a process clearly revealed in the Scots' own account of their origins. Though nowadays it is accepted that the occupancy of the British Isles by speakers of Celtic languages goes back much further into prehistory than was quite recently supposed, the Scots at least preserved the traditional knowledge or myth that they had come, as a people, to Ireland from somewhere else. What the Picts believed of their own origins has been lost, as has what the Britons of Strathclyde thought of theirs. (The Scots, for their own reasons, produced a theory of the Picts' origins, which the Britons also picked up on, and we will look at this.)

Even the Scots' account of their own beginnings, as we have it, is not an 'original' one. It has been heavily influenced by the need to adapt their traditional story, as they had preserved it up to the sixth century, to the demands of Christianity once they had been converted to the new religion. In essence, it is a genealogy, with some biographical and geographical details added. Like other such legends of early peoples, it traces the descent of the whole people, as a single kinship group, from a single ancestor of high prestige. In pagan times, this ancestor would have been a god (in the preserved Gaelic myths of the Ulster Cycle and others, there is still evidence of pseudohistorical kings and heroes fathered by Celtic gods). With the adoption of Christianity, a heathen pedigree was no longer acceptable, and a satisfactory alternative had to be found. The learned men found their model in the Bible narrative of the Old Testament, which itself is, among other things, a genealogical document of the Hebrew kings. If this was not the actual inspiration for the genealogies of Irish and Scottish kings, it certainly influenced them. The source was not so much the Bible, of which

St Jerome's Latin version, the Vulgate, had been completed in the late fourth century, as various commentators on the scriptural texts, such as the third-century Christian chronicler Eusebius, and his successors, Orosius in the sixth century and Isidore of Seville in the seventh. Eusebius, a Palestinian bishop whose Chronicon set out to synchronise events in Christian and pagan history, was especially influential on the way in which the various forms of the Annals were set out.

The earliest Old Irish texts do not survive, but many were still available in the twelfth century, when a collection of ancient Irish documents by various writers from different periods was put together in the *Lebor Gabála Érenn*, 'Book of the Taking of Ireland'. The scheme of the book is based on six successive invasions of, or arrivals in, Ireland.

The first is that of Cesair, granddaughter of Noah, sent to Ireland to escape the Flood. She is accompanied by her father, three other men, and 50 women. Their aim is to procreate and populate the land. Three hundred and twelve years later Partholón, also of Biblical stock, arrives. He and his people, the Partholonians, are descended from Magog. They settle in the east, but are ravaged by a plague. After a gap of 30 years, come Nemed and the Nemedians, from the region of the Caspian Sea. They settle more successfully than their predecessors, but they encounter a ferocious seaborne people called the Fomorians, noted as coming from the lands to the north of Ireland. The Fomorians establish their own colonies, doing battle with the Partholonians and the Nemedians. The fourth invasion is that of the Fir Bolg, the first people in the book to have a Celtic name ('men of Builg': a name probably cognate with that of the continental Celtic tribe of the Belgae), and said to have come many generations after the Nemedians. They are represented as short in stature and dark-haired. Thirty-seven years after them come the magic-endowed *Tuatha dé Danann*, 'people of the god Danann', a name that is still not satisfactorily explained. The Tuatha dé Danann defeat the Fir Bolg and the

Fomorians and institute the era in which much of early Irish myth and legend is set. The final invasion is that of the sons of Míl Espáine, literally 'soldier of Spain' and his eponymous followers the Milesians. Despite his name, Míl's career begins in the east, in Scythia, as a military leader. Later, in Egypt, he commands the armies of the pharaoh Nectanebo. He marries Scota, daughter of the pharaoh, and she bears him four sons, among them Éremon. In fulfilment of a druidic prophecy, they leave Egypt for the unknown island of Ireland, but stop off in Spain, the land of his birth. There he dies and Scota (whose name can mean 'Ireland' or 'Irishwoman') carries on to Ireland. Míl himself is taken as the direct ancestor of the Irish-Scottish Gaels, and their kings' genealogies stem from him. Éremon was the son of Scota and Míl, who ruled the northern half of Ireland, and to him the kings of Scots traced their own descent. A feature of their investitures was the recital of their pedigree back through Éremon and Míl to 'Eber the first Scot', grandson of Goídel Glas (see below), who was himself son of an earlier Scota. A genealogy of William I, king of Scots, from 1185, has been preserved, which does not stop even at Eber, but goes back another 23 generations before him, all the way to Noah (Skene, *Chronicles*).

It was, for a long time, assumed that at the basis of this ancient legend lay the real fact of a migration or migrations from a far-off eastern homeland to the new home in the furthest west. With the general abandonment by archaeologists of the idea of successive invasions, this assumption has in recent years seemed increasingly uncertain. There is a greater understanding of the way in which technology, belief, custom, and language could gradually spread without the need to be imported in a highly specific and sudden manner as the cultural baggage of warlike invaders. How, then, did the story of the invasions arise? The compilers of the *Lebor Gabála*, as has been noted, were heavily influenced by the Bible. There are strong echoes in their book of the story of the wanderings of the Israelites: their Egyptian sojourn, their wars, and their final establishment in a promised land. In addition, so as to be able to establish the Biblical pedigree of Irish-Scottish kings, it was essential to establish a link with the Israelites and with the part of the world they were known to inhabit. Coupled with the knowledge that such learned and semimagical techniques as iron-smelting and smithying had been passed on from an eastern source, it is possible at least to frame the outline of the way in which the migration story evolved.

The *Lebor Gabála* has been described as 'a laborious attempt to combine parts of the native teaching with Hebrew mythology embellished with medieval legend' (MacKillop). The bald outline is greatly elaborated and complicated with sometimes contradictory or anachronistic events. Elements from it are found in many other sources, often with differences of detail. The task, then, is to try to identify the real events which underlie the invasion stories.

Historians have discounted the first two 'invasions' of the *Lebor Gabála* as too obviously concocted back-projections by later writers. But the Nemedians are thought to have traces of historical truth mingled in the highly-coloured account of their battles with the Fomorians. And the latter, when stripped of mythological traits, and despite some anachronistic colouring by later scribes who knew the marauding Vikings, have been plausibly seen as inhabitants of the Western Isles, which show many signs of prehistoric habitation. Professor T. F. O'Rahilly identified the Nemedians with a prehistoric people he called the Érainn, speakers of a conjectured *p*-Celtic language (MacKillop, 304). In the *Lebor Gabála* the Nemedians are seen as the ancestors of the (Irish) *Cruithne* and of the *Bretnaigh Cluada*, 'Britons of Clyde'. The tentative linking of the Fir Bolg with the Belgae need not imply a heavy traffic between the dunes of Flanders and the sandy bays of southern Ireland; other related tribal names are found separated by wide stretches of territory – Damnonii in southern Scotland, Dumnonii in southwest England, for example. The semidivine Tuatha Dé are harder to relate to any set of real people; they represent rather an idealised era which ends fittingly, in one tale anyway, when on their defeat by the Milesians they retire to Tir na nOg, the mythical land of the ever-young. In other versions they retreat underground, in the many barrows and raths of the Irish landscape, and their race becomes that of the fairy folk. The Milesians are the first overtly Gaelic-speaking people to be mentioned. Part of their story indeed is the creation of Gaelic, after the Biblical Tower of Babel episode, by Goídel Glas, on the instructions of his grandfather, Fénius Farsaid. Goídel Glas, his name later found as Gathelus, was son of Niúl, and – like the later Míl Espáine – his mother was Scota, a pharaoh's daughter. In one of the clever inserted links that help to give the story plausibility, Goídel's by-name of *Glas*, 'green', refers to a mark left by a snakebite. He was cured of this in Egypt by Moses, who also prophesied that his descendants would one day live in a country where no snakes were to be found. And, sure enough, Ireland is well-known for its lack of snakes . . .

Also found at a later stage in the Milesian story, when they have reached Ireland, is their encounter with three goddesses, each of whom asks the Milesians to name Ireland after her: Banba, Ériu, and Fódla. These names are closely identified with the land of the Gaels. Ériu is preserved in Erin, and also, according to some toponymists, in Earn and Strathearn – seen as names given by Scottish colonists in Pictish territory; Banba has (more dubiously) been seen in the name Banff; while Fódla is seen in the name Atholl, as 'ford of Fódla'. Not the least interesting aspect of the Milesian story is the implication that the speakers of Gaelic came to an Ireland that was Celtic-speaking, but of a *p*-Celtic language. In the words of professor James MacKillop, referring to political power:

'Milesian hegemony spread to all corners of Ireland.' (*Dictionary of Celtic Mythology*)

From a modest start in the sixth century, the descendants of Goídel Glas and Míl would achieve the same result in Scotland.

The Scots, of course, were relative newcomers to Scotland, compared with the Picts and the Britons. In Ireland, their roots went back as far as memory and imagination could stretch; as colonists in Pictland, they were upstarts. Awareness of this is likely to have coloured their own versions of history, including the history of other peoples. Bede, writing more than two hundred years after the arrival of the Dàl Riata, relates a story about the origin of the Picts that he has clearly picked up from the Scots:

> '. . . it is said some Picts from Scythia put to sea in a few longships, and were driven by storms around the coasts of Britain, arriving at length on the north coast of Ireland. Here they found the nation of the Scots, from whom they asked permission to settle, but their request was refused . . . The Scots replied that there was not room for them both, but said: "We can give you good advice. There is another island not far to the east, which we often see in the distance on clear days. Go and settle there if you wish; should you meet resistance, we will come to your help." So the Picts crossed into Britain, and began to settle in the north of the island, since the Britons were in possession of the south. Having no women with them, these Picts asked wives of the Scots, who consented on condition that, when any dispute arose, they should choose a king from the female royal line rather than the male. This tradition continues among the Picts to this day.' (Bede, I, i)

This famous tale is found in a number of different versions in old Irish writings. It has two fireworks figuratively attached to it: the suggestion that the Picts owe their habitat and their continuing existence as a people to the Scots; and the implication that they, in the case of 'disputes', chose their kings on the

basis of descent from the mother and not, as with the Scots
themselves and every other recorded society in Western Europe, from the father. The 15th-century *Book of Lecain* specifically links these points to the assertion that: ' . . . of the men of
Erin has been the chieftainship over Cruthentuath from that
time ever since' (Skene, *Chronicles*). The Britons added their
own twist by fostering a version of the story that states that the
Picts first came to them, as a roving Scythian war band that
fought and was defeated by them, before asking for wives. But
'the Britons would not marry their daughters to foreigners of
another country without knowing of what race they were, and
aliens they were, moreover, and they refused their petition,
and after their refusal they went to Ireland, and married
women of the Gael' (Skene, *Chronicles*, 122–23). This version
neatly established the Britons at the top of the 'We were here
first' debate – not just a prestige point, but a significant position in matters such as land and boundary disputes.

'Scythian', incidentally, was a generic term as ethnically and
geographically indistinct as Celtic; it referred to the inhabitants
of a vast swathe of northern Europe from the Black Sea to the
Norwegian fiords, and its use does not shed much light on the
origins of the Picts. The Gaelic name for Pict is *Cruithne*,
which, in *qu*-Celtic form, is cognate with the Old Welsh *Priteni*.
Both terms originally meant an inhabitant of North Britain,
and not specifically a Pict. The Gaels knew of Cruithne before
any of them set sail across the North Channel. Sharing the
north Ulster coastland with the Dàl Riata was a people known
as being of the race of Cruithne, whose tribal name by the sixth
century CE was the Dàl Araidhe. Although regarded as a subject
people by the Ulster Gaels, the Dàl Araidhe sometimes succeeded in possessing the overkingship of the province. There
was also a group known as the Cruithin, established in Meath,
in the centre of Ireland. These are generally understood to be
the same people as the Caledonian Picts, and to have entered
Ireland at an unknown time from North Britain. Possibly,

though, the movement was in the other direction. There is a lingering account, found in several different ancient sources, that the Picts came into North Britain from the north, settling first in Orkney and spreading south from there. This does not fit badly with the notion of a departure from the northern coast of Ireland, via the Western Isles. Intriguing as these matters are, they have been shelved or ignored by historians for lack of convincing evidence to support any particular theory. Even the language of the Dàl Araidhe has a question mark over it. Was it Pictish? Had it been Pictish and been supplanted by Gaelic? What were the relations between those Irish-located Cruithne and their Pictish neighbours across the narrow sea, the nearest being the Epidii of Kintyre, identified by Ptolemy in 150CE but unheard of since?

Although no Pictish tale of origins is preserved, we do have, from a tenth-century Scottish document, the so-called 'Pictish Chronicle'. This combines a brief account (taken from Isidore of Seville, a great rehasher of legendary information) of the 'history of the ancient Picts', together with a sequence of Pictish kings and their reign lengths, and occasional brief items of information relating to a particular king or reign. It also comprises a list of kings from Kenneth MacAlpin to Kenneth II – this is clearly not from a Pictish source. The Pictish king list begins with Cruithne son of Cinge, 'father of the Picts living in this island, who reigned 100 years'. It then lists his seven sons, Fib, Fidach, Floclaid, Fortrenn, Got [Cat], Ce, and Circinn. Circinn is noted as the first to reign after Cruithne, followed by the others as listed, except that Fib takes his place at the end. This transposition was taken by W. F. Skene, to show that the document was written at Brechin, in the province of Angus (the earlier Circinn) – the scribe wanted to claim pre-eminence for his own region.

There follow 69 kings until Bridei son of Maelcon, who is nowadays regarded as the first demonstrably historical king of the Picts, as his name and dates are corroborated in other sources. The earlier kings, and especially those earlier than Nectan Morbet, who is credited with the foundation of the priory at Abernethy, are regarded as increasingly fictional, though their names have provided a ready source of speculation for anyone trying to find bottom in the dark pool of Pictish mythology and history.

Most scholars would, however, agree with Euan MacKie that: 'The archaeological evidence, though sparse . . . is increasingly suggesting that the majority of the Picts were descended from the Iron Age, or even the Late Bronze Age tribes of the same area' (*Scotland*, 31).

Impressive and suggestive as the ancient Irish legends are – one of the oldest literatures of Europe – there are few reliable facts that can be extracted from them. Only archaeology can establish definite knowledge of the prehistoric period. The basic forms of the Scots' legendary history can then be compared with the modern explanation arrived at by the accrued work of historians, antiquarians, linguists, and, latterly, archaeologists, between the 14th and the 21st centuries. Needless to say, the process has not been a smoothly progressive one; it has been marked by storms of controversy and prejudice, brilliantly documented in William Ferguson's *The Identity of the Scottish Nation*.

Languages of North Britain and Caledonia

The question of language origin remains. Despite the preservation of the migration legend, and the long-established general view that the ancestral form of the western Celtic languages came from the East, at least one distinguished Celtic scholar has found it possible to support the suggestion that the Celts originated in Ireland. The archaic nature of theIrish Gaelic language is mentioned in this context, as are structural remains and the evidence of ancient cults such as that of head-hunting.

'Ireland, then is an attractive and perhaps tempting choice
for the ultimate place of origin for the complex and highly-
talented, war-mad peoples whom, for the sake of conve-
nience, we term "the Celts".' (Anne Ross, *The Druids*)

The further ramifications and consequences of the idea are not
explored, however. Most Celtic scholars, however, accept the
view that the 'Common Celtic' language originated in south
central Europe, and that its descendant tongues spread from
there, not necessarily by means of large-scale migration. As we
will see below, important questions on the history of the Celtic
languages remain unresolved, and with them, questions on the
location of different groups of 'Celtic' peoples.

The question of language is important since, as the Irish
philologist, Myles Dillon, made clear, the acceptance of long
residence by Celtic speakers in Ireland and Britain should
mean acceptance of the view that the change in the Gaulish
and Brittonic languages from *qu-* to *p-*happened during this
period, when speakers of a Celtic language were already living
in Ireland. Dillon saw such speech innovations spreading from
a centre on the continent and failing to reach as far as the 'lat-
eral' areas of Ireland and Spain, where the old forms remained
in use. But there is evidence of *p*-Celtic speakers in Ireland
from early times. How did the Gaels fail to adopt this change,
if they lived amidst people who did? Were the Gaels, or rather
proto-Gaels, somewhere else at the time? Was that somewhere
else located in the Iberian peninsula (whose Celtiberian language is considered to have been *qu*-Celtic)? Such questions
remain unanswerable, at least until further concrete evidence
is produced in the form of comparable texts or word samples.
Other questions remain linked to the Celtic language of the
Picts, which, as has been noted, was more akin to continental
Gaulish than to insular Brittonic. Unfortunately, the remnants
of both Gaulish and Pictish are so slight that it is impossible to
build much on this similarity. It can be used both to sustain the

'invasion' theory – that the leading elements of Pictish society came, perhaps in the first century, from Gaul – and the 'indigenous' theory – that, in its remote region, the Pictish language did not pick up the changes that came to characterise Brittonic.

International Relations

Contacts between Celtic societies were well established from ancient times. Exploration of the rich continental Celtic burial sites, whose artefacts are characterised as being in the La Tène, and earlier the Hallstatt, style, has made it clear that, for the Celtic peoples, trading and diplomacy with groupings of other peoples was a regular procedure. The chieftaincies of the Hallstatt culture and the warrior aristocracies of the La Tène period both grew rich by occupying pivotal points on north-south communication routes in middle Europe. The tribes who lived north of Hadrian's Wall were not outside this system, though they represented the end of the trading–line, rather than a junction or toll point. In the Roman period, their southward forays each time a Roman governor was replaced show that they were informed of what was happening within the Roman province.

The famous 'coordinated' attack by Picts, Scots, and Attacotti in 367 suggests that there were means of arranging for joint action and for making it effective. Such operations require a good deal of liaison. The organisation of trade and the exchange of goods can be relatively easily understood, especially if the role of middlemen is granted. There is evidence in gravestone inscriptions of Greek and Syrian traders operating as far north as Hadrian's Wall during the Roman occupancy. Wherever there were numbers of troops on a regular payroll, the traders would follow, no matter how remote and exotic the location.

The means of diplomatic contact between peoples are much less apparent. In the cadre of professionals within the tribes, 'diplomats' are not included as a group. Such roles were encompassed by people classified in other ways, but presumably drawn from the ranks of the druids (later priests) and the bards and historians. Men in these cadres were members of leading families and possessed the necessary prestige, knowledge, and authority. The freedom of passage granted to members of these orders may have been more a recognition of their diplomatic work than of their artistic abilities. Mastering of other languages was an essential part of this work, since communication was oral (language-learning might be a useful by-product of fostering or hostage-taking, at least when the hostage survived). The achievement of treaties and agreements might be recorded in various ways, as by the exchange of symbolic objects and gifts, but the details do not seem to have been written down.

Although he should be considered a special case, we see Columcille acting in this sort of capacity at the 'Synod' of Drum Ceatt, in 575, where difficult negotiations between the two Dàl Riadas, and between Dàl Riada and Ulster, had to be carried on. He is likely to have been a prime mover in setting this up, rather than a delegate of one side or another. Emissaries and adjudicators were necessary to deal with other intertribal matters such as royal marriages, the giving of hostages, the ransoming of prisoners, and the exchange of gifts. Arranging the details of military cooperation and coordination would seem to require a different set of skills, but the same high level of communication abilities.

Perhaps in matters such as this, the regular practice of seeking to make royal marriage arrangements beyond the tribe again has a part to play. Relations between cousin- or even brother-kings were by no means necessarily always friendly but, when they were amicable, the family link must have eased the potential difficulties of cooperation by providing an umbrella of joint royal patronage, under which mutually suspicious subchiefs could meet and discuss the mechanics of alliance and of joint attack or defence.

The missionary aspect of Christianity brought a kind of contact between peoples. The Dàl Riadan colonists were already

Christians and, from early in the sixth century, determined missions to convert the Picts to Christianity were under way. Following the efforts of the Briton, St Patrick (thought to have come from a prominent family in the Romano-British city of Carlisle), his predecessors and his successors (he died around 461), many of the Irish tribal kingdoms had adopted Christianity. The custodians of their bardic and druidic traditions had come to terms with the new religion and, to a degree, Christianity had absorbed parts of the old tradition. It is not clear how far the first Hebridean monasteries were mission stations and how far they were simply religious communities founded in 'desert' places, where the monks could pursue their austere avocations in peace. But a strong teaching and missionary purpose was evident from the fifth century at least, and considerable progress had been made.

The king of Strathclyde, Rhydderch, was a Christian. The Picts, it seems, were still pagan, yet in his lifetime St Patrick had written of 'apostate Picts', who bought Christians as slaves (*Letter to Coroticus*). This suggests that some, at least, had accepted Christianity and then reverted to paganism. Who or where these apostate Picts were is not known. But it seems likely that fifth-century missionaries from Whithorn took their message into Pictish territory, and established churches in some places in the name of their own founder, Ninian. These isolated churches may not have survived, and required refounding in the course of the Christian expansion of the sixth and seventh centuries. It is notable that a string of churches dedicated to St Ninian follows the eastern coastline all the way up to Shetland, a long way from Whithorn. Ninian had no connection with Iona, and a missionary venture originating from Iona would not have had any reason to use his name. Despite the hostile rivalry between the druid Broichan and Columcille, described by Adamnan in his *Life of St Columba*, the Picts appear to have been relatively tolerant in religious matters. Although St Columba did not convert king

Bridei to Christianity, he was allowed to preach and to send evangelising monks into Pictland. The inference is that individuals could adopt Christianity, even though the official cult was still that of the druids. But once the king was converted, Christianity became the 'state' religion.

In the early years of the sixth century, the first stages of such missionary efforts must have seemed a minor affair to those who ruled the affairs of Pictland. Looking out at the wider scene, they would have known of the successful Saxon invasions in the far south of Britain and perceived that Saxon kingdoms were being formed. By 547, the Angles had established a small but tenacious kingdom, Bernicia, on the coastal fringe around Bamburgh, just south of the Tweed estuary. The erstwhile raiding allies were becoming settlers and the raiding grounds were consequently shrinking. Still, a great phalanx of British tribal areas and kingdoms stretched between Pictland and the uncertain frontiers of the Germanic colonists. Strathclyde itself was a strong and vigorous kingdom whose southern frontier was that of Cumbria. The terrible Roman legions were receding into vivid legend. Hadrian's Wall was crumbling. There was no emperor in the West. Gaul was being contested by great tribal groups from east of the Rhine: Franks, Vandals, Goths. Constantinople was a world away.

However great the flux of domestic events, it must have appeared to be a world of largely stable elements, with Pictland itself as a significant part. From around 556 to 586, the first historically,proven king of Picts, Bridei, son of Maelcon, maintained a long reign, from a royal site at Inverness. Maelcon has been linked to Maelgwyn, king of Gwynedd, in the northern part of Wales, but the similarity of names and the coincidence of dates are the only evidence for this. From Adamnan's *Life of St Columba*. we know that Bridei was ruler or overlord of Orkney, through a *regulus*, or petty king. Evidently, his domain stretched as far as Dàl Riada to the southwest. Whether it encompassed the entire territory of

Pictland, particularly the southeastern provinces of Strathearn, Atholl, Fife, and Angus, we do not know. In the Pictish king lists, a hazy figure recorded as Galam Cennalaph is said to have reigned before Bridei for four years; one version says that he and Bridei reigned for one year together. The 'Annals of Ulster', calling him Cennalaph, say he died only a few years before Bridei, in 579. This scanty information may indicate that Cennalaph ruled a separate region; or that he was deposed and replaced by Bridei.

Pictland was indeed to remain stable; perhaps its internal cohesion even increased at this time, with a single kingship controlling its mainland and island territories. In many ways, across a generation, its world may have appeared changeless, especially to those who took or were allowed no interest in the wider picture. But, by the end of the sixth century, events had taken place that would have a profound influence on the Picts in the decades to come.

In 540, the British ecclesiastic, Gildas, wrote a text intended, not as a history or description, but as a moral tract for those in charge of his own society, including Maelgwyn of Gwynedd, possible father of the Pictish king Bridei. Some choice uncomplimentary epithets are reserved for Maelgwyn – Gildas was no respecter of persons. He also makes vituperative reference to the Picts and Scots, as '. . . foul hordes . . . like dark throngs of worms who wriggle out of narrow fissures in the rock when the sun is high and the weather grows warm.' Gildas may have been a native of the southwest, or of Wales. Much of his account is backward-looking but it clearly implies that relations between the kingdoms were not good. Strathclyde and the other British kingdoms to its south had a bitter struggle on their hands against the Angles both of Bernicia and of its neighbouring kingdom of Deira in what is now central and eastern Yorkshire, and their efforts to drive the newcomers back into the sea were a failure. Inexorably the Angles pushed their frontiers out into British territory.

Aethelfrith, king of Bernicia from 593, became king also of Deira and united the two territories in the large expansion-minded kingdom of Northumbria. He was master of all the land between Humber and Tweed. The rise of Northumbria intensified the Britons' efforts to hold their own territories. The poem 'Y Gododdin', ascribed to the Cumbric-speaking sixth-century bard, Aneirin, tells of a heroic but disastrous assault on Catraeth (now Catterick) in Deira by a band of 300 warriors, mostly of the Gododdin (Votadini) tribe, sent by their king Mynyddog Mwynfawr, 'the wealthy', from his fortress in Lothian, which may have been sited on what later became the Castle Rock of Edinburgh:

'From men who had been mead-nourished and wine-nourished
A bright array charged forth, who had drunk together from the bowl.
For the feast in the mountain stronghold they were to perish –
Too many I have lost of my true kinsmen.
Of the the three hundred gold-torqued men who attacked Catraeth,
Alas! Only one escaped.'

Defeat was more frequent than victory for the Britons in the prolonged struggle. The Picts and Scots appear to have remained largely aloof from this conflict.

The Kingdom of Dàl Riada

After some 50 years of peaceful consolidation of their position, the Scots had spread across Argyll and the southern Hebrides. They were grouped in three tribal divisions, whose names reflect the tradition of Fergus and his brothers Oengus and Loarn: the Cineal Oengus, centred on Islay and Jura; the Cineal

Loairn in the district still called Lorn, with Dunstaffnage and Dunollie as its two main fortresses; and the Cineal Gabhrain, called after Gabhràn, grandson of Fergus, and comprising Kintyre, Knapdale, Bute, and Arran, with the rock of Dunadd as one key point, if not its principal one. With the Cineal Gabhrain was also associated the Cineal Comgal, named for Gabhràn's brother who had preceded him as king; and still traceable in the district name of Cowal, with Dunoon still its capital. The Gaelic word *cineal* means 'offspring' or 'race': the descendants. Its use reflects a primarily genealogical record, but the heads of these groups, as subkings, would possess substantial autonomy within the laws of Irish society and the prerogatives of the senior king. This kingship in the first generations was to remain exclusive to Fergus's family, the Cineal Gabhrain.

By now, the Scottish colony was certainly large enough to impinge upon its neighbours, and Gabhràn himself, who became king of Dàl Riada in 539, seems to have been the first king of the Scots to make an impact on the neighbouring lands. It would be customary for the kings of adjacent regions to exchange courtesies of various sorts as acknowledgment of each other's status. These would include gifts and royal marriages. Friendly relations might be cemented by sending kings' sons or nephews as fosterlings. Acknowledgment of a neighbouring king's greater power might be marked by the giving of hostages. By one or more of these means, Gabhràn had formed strong links with the Pictish country to the east. It is possible that the Pictish territory south of the Grampians, which included Gowrie and Fife, was divided into separate kingdoms, which owed little or no allegiance to the king at Inverness. In examining the etymology of the district name, Gowrie, W. J. Watson links it to Gabhràn, and surmises that Gabhràn married into a Pictish ruling family of that district and himself was given the land of Gowrie as 'Gabhràn's land', before he returned to become king of the Scots on the death of his brother, Comgall (Watson, 112). Relations between the

Scots and the Picts, at a high social level, thus go back to early days. The drive of the Dàl Riadan Scots towards territorial expansion may represent their sense of occupying a 'beach-head' position on the Scottish mainland; the insecurity of this gave them a sense of impetus that the sixth-century Picts, living in vast territories occupied since time immemorial, did not have. In this there may be a contribution to the Scots' ultimate dominance of the country. During Gabhràn's kingship, whether simply by their own prolific breeding, or reinforced by further arrivals from Ulster, or because of expanding territorial claims, the numbers of the Scots and the amount of territory they were now occupying began to disturb the northern Pictish king, Bridei. In 559 or 560, he came down with his army through the Great Glen and into Lorn, defeating the Scots in battle and forcing them back, perhaps as far as the River Add. Gabhràn was killed in this war and his nephew Conall assumed the kingship.

Columcille

It was thus at a time of an assertive and suspicious Pictish monarchy that the Scots monk Columcille, already famed and to some notorious in Ireland, arrived in Dàl Riada in 563, accompanied, tradition has it, by twelve followers. Conall allowed him to settle on an island then known as Hinba (perhaps Jura, or the much smaller Eilean nan Naoimh, of the Garvellachs). Here he established a monastery. It is likely that the monastic community on Iona, not far away, had already been founded, perhaps by St Oran, some decades before; it was by tradition already the royal burial ground, where Fergus MacErc and his sons had been interred, and probably had been a sacred place in pagan times. Some time after 563, Columcille became abbot of the Iona monastery. By this time in his early 40s, he was a man in his prime, immensely energetic, a commanding personality, poet, and scholar, of Úi Néill royal blood

himself, whose undoubted religious zeal and personal asceticism did not deter him from setting his hand to temporal matters, In some ways he resembled St Ambrose, the fifth-century
bishop of Milan, also a writer of hymns, who was able to subject the most powerful man in the world, the emperoror
Theodosius, to the discipline of the Church.

The Irish Church, though it maintained relations with
Rome, and acknowledged the status of the pope as St Peter's
successor, was not under his authority, nor did it have a centralised hierarchy of its own. When pope Honorius I wrote to
it in 640, to commend the Roman Easter observance, he was
careful to exhort rather than to command, and his letter was
addressed severally to numerous bishops and abbots. The Irish
Church would certainly have considered itself part of the universal Church, as its missionary efforts show. But it reflected
the society in which it had developed. Its organisation was par-
allel to that of the tribes, and its bishops were pastors to the
tuath, rather than to a territory. None had the formal authority
of a metropolitan, and it was the saintliness and other personal
attributes of a bishop or abbot that determined his wider influence. This close link between ruling families and bishops
harks back to the old pagan tradition of the priest-king, and
does not simply mean a political extension of royal control
into a new sphere; numerous kings of Scots and of Picts would
retire into monastic life.

Iona is nowadays seen as a remote and peripheral island but,
in the sixth century, its position was central among the sea
routes of the Gaelic-speaking tribes. In a few years, it was
established as the chief spiritual centre of the Irish Church, its
offshore location and Columcille's particular semidetached
status from the internal struggles of Ireland combining to
assist its progress. The towering stature of Columcille among
the churchmen and rulers of his time is chiefly the result of his
own achievement. But he was fortunate in having an assidu-
ous biographer 100 years after his death, whose work has been

preserved. Adamnan, ninth abbot of Iona in line from
Columba, wrote a Latin *Life* of the saint, which is a valuable
source of information on many aspects of the later sixth century. But its avowed purpose is to glorify a great saint, and not
to provide a measured record of his life and deeds. The light
thus projected on Columcille has deepened the shade in which
many of his contemporary missionaries are cast and has caused
at times a kind of anti-Columban backlash among Church historians, suggesting that the Columban cult has deliberately
ignored the work of such as St Ninian, St Blane, St Serf, St
Luoc, St Colman, St Fillan, and others who worked independently in Pictland before and during his time. Although it was
claiming to do proper justice to the contribution of the other
missionaries, this school of thought was not free from anti-
Irish prejudice. Dr William Ferguson has recorded the reluc-
tance of many Scottish writers, from the 16th to the 19th
centuries, to accept the validity of their country's Irish inheritance. The 'Scottish' Ninian was preferred to the 'Irish'
Columba. Though he is recorded as having preached among
the Picts (through an interpreter), Columba himself undertook
little missionary activity. After his death, inspired by his life and
the miraculous stories already gathering around his name,
Ionan missionaries spread through Pictland.

The developing structure of the Church followed the
model of social structure, as had happened in Ireland. It has
been noted that, after the events of 843, it was necessary to
make the practices of the Pictish and Scottish Churches conform to each other. This may have been because of the diver-
gences that happened in the eighth century, but there is
nothing to suggest that, following the conversion of the Picts,
the Pictish Church was part of the Scottish one. The establishment of a Church and its endowment would require the consent of a Pictish king or chieftain and be governed by Pictish
law and custom. Although Iona remained the most influential
religious centre, and by tradition a burial place for Pictish as

well as Scottish kings, it would have been natural for the
Pictish Church to have been formed in line with the Picts'
own tribal divisions, for the Pictish king to play an important
role in it, and for its bishops and clergy to fulfil some of the
secular functions of the druids whom they replaced.

Kings

Harmony did not prevail among the three groupings of the
Scots, and Conall's kingship appears to have been an uneasy
one. The Cineal Loairn had been thrust back and were
unlikely to accept their defeat as the last word. The northern
boundary with the Picts remained in dispute. There were differences with the overking of Ulster over the dues payable by
the Dàl Riadan Scots as his subjects. Columcille's natural
authority was exercised in these matters. His visit to the
Pictish king in 565 had a diplomatic as well as a religious purpose (some recent writers have suggested that this visit was
not, in fact, made until ten years later, in 575). Shorn of the
miraculous details related by Adamnan, the mission to Bridei,
if it happened in 565, may have been a political necessity to
assure Iona's security, following the Pictish victory over the
Scots in 560. On the religious front, Bridei agreed to permit
evangelical work in his lands, though he and his advisers did
not accept Christianity themselves. Columcille was given
leave for one of his followers, Cormac, to land in Orkney and,
from this account, we know that at Bridei's court there was a
subking of Orkney, from whom Bridei held hostages, making
it clear that Orkney was under Pictish rule or suzerainty
(Adamnan, 169). How successful the saint's diplomatic mission was is not clear.

Abbot Columcille spoke Gaelic; king Bridei spoke Pictish.
They conversed through an interpreter, presumably one of
Columcille's team. Adamnan also records the Picts 'hearing
the word of life through an interpreter when the holy man

preached', so interpreters were needed not only for the careful details of official conversations but for all forms of communication.

Conall died in 574 and warfare broke out for the succession. Columcille's influence was put behind Aedan, son of Gabhràn, in preference to his elder brother Eoganan. Aedan became king. Partly by analogy with the better-recorded Irish pattern from which they emerged, and partly through such Scottish records as the *Senchus fer nAlban*, 'History of the Men of Alba', a document from the tenth century, but using information compiled in the late seventh century, the organisation of the Scots is much better known than that of the Picts. They were a homogeneous group; there never appears to been any suggestion that they 'absorbed' Picts previously living in the territory. (But what became of the Epidii, the tribe noted by Ptolemy as occupying Kintyre in the second century, and whose name implies *p*-Celtic language speakers? Nothing is known of them or their fate, though it has been noted that 'horse' names were prominent there in Gaelic times, as in MacEachern, 'son of the horse lord').

As we have already seen, the Scots who colonised Argyll and the inner isles divided into three main tribal groups: the Cineal Gabhrain, the Cineal Loairn, and the Cineal Aonghus, with each occupying a distinct district. From the Cineal Gabhrain also emerged the Cineal Comghall of Cowal. Each of these *cinele* had a chief, or king (Gaelic *righ*). One of these kings was also the overking of the Dàl Riata. For many years, the size and prestige of the Cineal Gabhrain meant that its king was the overking. Below the kings, in each *cineal*, were further area chiefs, at the head of island or mainland communities, and below them were the heads of individual families within the kin group. Each of these leaders had his share of authority within his domain, and each owed loyalty to his next chief and the king. All shared a history, religious beliefs, a language, and a range of social customs and traditions. To the overking were due certain duties and payments of tribute from all the subkingdoms. The duties included military service both by land and sea, with each household assessed for its contribution. The *Senchus fer nAlban* shows that a king who mustered the Dàl Riadan forces had a precise idea of how many households his subkings controlled and the number of fighting men they should provide. It was not a haphazard business. One can picture his captain counting them off at the muster, rank by rank and boat by boat.

Kings were made, not born, albeit from a narrow section of society. This was the *derbfine*, consisting of all the men who could claim descent up to the third generation from a king – a range of brothers, cousins, uncles, and nephews whose numbers could rise into double figures if a king were long-lived. The competition among them could and often did make for strife within the *cineal*. In the case of the choice of an overking, the *derbfine* of the incumbent would provide the candidates. But here, the choice might be challenged or repudiated by another of the *cinele*, either for personal reasons of opposition or because it sought to install its own man. The long tenure of the overkingship by the Cineal Gabhrain seems to have been increasingly resented by the other main kindred groups of the Dàl Riata. Relations between these groups were often hostile and frequently broke out in open warfare. The Cineal Loairn, squeezed between its own kindred to the south and Pictish territory to the north, was often restive. It may have been its efforts to expand northwards that brought Bridei's Picts down on the Scots in 550. The foot-shaped indentation in the stone surface of Dunadd is often taken as the mark of a place where kings were inaugurated. Setting the new king's foot here was assumed to be part of the ceremony. This is quite likely, but although Dunadd was plainly an important fort, there is no evidence to prove that it was the royal centre of Dàl Riada: it may have been the headquarters of a subking.

After Kenneth MacAlpin, the kings of Scots were inaugurated on the moot hill of Scone, which may have been used for

the same purpose by the Pictish kings of Fortriu. Details of the
ritual used at Scone, including the seating of the king upon the
Stone of Destiny, and the recital of his pedigree, all come from
a later period than that covered by this book. Though events
like the crowning of Alexander III in the open air outside
Scone Abbey in 1249, may well have been modelled on well-
known and long-established precedents, we do not have any
details. But it seems likely that, until the ninth century, the
Stone of Destiny, brought across from Ireland as a sacred possession of the Dàl Riata, was kept at Dunstaffnage, not at
Dunadd.

Soon after Aedan's accession, a battle was fought at a place
called Delgon in Kintyre; a son of Conall was killed, together
with 'many others of the race of Gabhràn'. The implication is
a defeat for the Scots, though the enemy is not recorded. It
may have been a Pyrrhic victory for the Cineal Gabhrain in an
internecine struggle with another group. Aedan was a notable
warrior-king, even in an age when battle prowess was a king's
chief attribute. With Columcille as his counsellor, he went to
Ireland in 575 to attend a kind of 'summit meeting' of Irish
kings, bishops, and abbots at Drum Ceatt, convened by Aedh,
high king of Ireland. At this, an accommodation was reached
between the king of Scots and the king of Ulster: rents and
tributes would no longer be paid, though the Dàl Riadan Scots
remained under a pledge to give military service. The effect of
Drum Ceatt was to confirm the kingdom of the Scots as a separate entity and no longer an Irish colony. At this time, the
Irish Dàl Riata remained under the rule of the Scottish king.

Territorial Wars

There may have been others before, but the first territorial
wars recorded on Scottish soil begin with the establishment
of the Scots and their efforts to expand north and south.
Interestingly, their extension in an eastwards direction does

not appear to have caused trouble at first. But the movement of the Cineal Loairn up into the Great Glen brought war with the Inverness-based Picts; and the Scots' frontier war with the Strathclyde Britons, fought in Glen Falloch and across the wild mountainous country that lies between it and Loch Awe, ended badly for the Scots, with the Britons occupying a large extent of Dàl Riada. The systems of providing for royal succession in both Pictland and Dàl Riada broke down occasionally through dispute, with warfare resulting. The effects of this are recorded in the history of Dàl Riada, with the struggles of Cineal Loairn to provide a king, and its own internal strife when it succeeded. They are also clearly seen in the succession of battles between Pictish contenders that ended with the emergence of Oengus in 729.

Dr Nora Chadwick, in *The Celts*, makes an important point in distinguishing between 'essential' and 'nonessential' aspects of war. Where territory was not threatened, she remarks: 'This type of warfare had characteristics more akin to those of hunting than to true wars of aggression or defence.' She links this to the tradition of Gaelic legend, especially the famous *Táin Bó Cuailnge*, or 'Cattle Raid of Cooley', and the exploits of the educated young warriors of the Fianna. The young men of the 'warrior' class, with plenty of energy and nothing productive to do, needed exercise. The raid, designed to lift cattle or slaves, appears to have been a well-established tradition in the societies of third-century Scotland. It was the slave-raiding by the Picts that St Patrick expostulated against in his letter to Coroticus; 100 years later, Columba saw a Scots slave girl at the court of king Bridei. Some writers believe that a newly created king or subking was required by tradition to lead his hunter-warriors off on a raid whose success would make an auspicious beginning to his reign (a practice certainly known in the Highlands until the 16th century). Such activities were very different from warfare. In the early years of the fifth century, Gildas complains that the Picts are unwilling to face proper warfare, meaning a

Roman army, and he was undoubtedly right. Their deep raids into Britannia in the fifth century were entirely opportunistic, based on the lack of defence within the Roman provinces at that time.

In 580, Aedan is recorded as leading an expedition by sea to Orkney. This need not have been to fight the Picts; it has been suggested that he could have gone as an ally to help put down a rising, though it could just as easily have been to support one. It seems an odd location for an expedition by the Scots. Bridei was still king of Pictland and there is no reason to suppose his grip on the north was less secure than before. In the south of Pictland, it was a different matter. In 584, Bridei was killed in battle in the southern province of Circinn (Angus), fighting against other Picts. This event suggests either that Bridei was fighting to assert his rights, which were not currently being honoured, or that he was trying to establish rights that may not previously have existed. Dynastic war in southern Pictland would certainly be of interest to Aedan macGabhràn, with his inherited interest in Gowrie. Although the sources are obscure, it seems that he campaigned in the east. Adamnan in a dramatic scene recounts how St Columba suddenly told his servant Diormit to summon the clergy to the church: 'Now let us pray to the Lord earnestly for this people and King Aedan; for in this hour they are entering battle.' It was recorded as 'the battle of the Miathi', a name that corresponds to the Maeatae, and suggests that the tribal or federative name was still current 400 years after it was first noted. It would seem that Aedan was fighting in Pictland, either against or in alliance with, Pictish factions. The battle ended in victory, though two of Aedan's sons were killed; but none of Aedan's campaigns appear to have won territory for the Scots.

He also met a new enemy. For the first time, Gael faced Teuton in battle. During the last years of the sixth century, the Angles of Northumbria had been pushing further north. The kingdom of the Gododdin was steadily overrun until, by the end of the sixth century, the Northumbrians' northern frontier was on the Forth, and the Celtic inhabitants of the old Votadini lands were either fled, dead, or absorbed into the new Germanic kingdom.

In 603, Aedan attacked the Angles at a place called Degsastan – a locality which has not been fixed, though Dawston in Liddesdale has been suggested – and was heavily defeated by an army led by king Aethelfrith. The Scots withdrew from further confrontation. Only the Britons of Strathclyde held out against the Northumbrians, not without loss of territory. By 613, the Northumbrians had crossed the gap between the Tyne and Carlisle, and controlled the land from coast to coast. Some time between 613 and 616, under Aethelfrith, they won a significant victory over the Britons at Chester. The north Britons were now separated from the south Britons, each group surrounded by acquisitive neighbours on land, and with a coastline exposed to the raids of the Irish. In the space of a lifetime, Northumbria had risen to be the most powerful kingdom in Britain, and its expansion was not yet over.

In 597, Columcille died, but his great prestige and the monastery's established role ensured that Iona remained the spiritual centre of the church. Bridei, king of the Picts, whom the saint may have visited on more than one occasion, had been succeeded by Gartnait, and he by Nechtan in 599. By this time, it seems that the centre of Pictish kingship had moved south, into Angus or Strathearn. Several reasons have been put forward for this shift. It may reflect a political need to control a province with overindependent rulers. Perhaps it shows the expansion of a set of family interests based originally in the north, or the opposite – the rise of a southern family eclipsing a northern one. The southern frontier of the Picts was clearly at risk, and may have required the authority and resources of the king to help maintain it.

There was a further good reason. To Pictish strategists, the threat of a northward push from the Cineal Loairn must have seemed a minor one compared to the strong eastward-bearing pressures led by Aedan towards Atholl, Strathearn, and Strathmore. The name of Atholl, not only Gaelic but proclaiming an identity of 'New Ireland' (Watson), first noted from 739, shows a Scottish identity proclaimed in a Pictish province long before Kenneth MacAlpin's time; and we have already noted the apparent macGabhràn interest in the adjacent district of Gowrie. At a time when the southern Picts were not unified, the Scots appear to have made substantial inroads in these regions.

The power and effectiveness of the Pictish monarchy may have fluctuated, as also happened with the kingship of Scots and the overkingships of Ireland. A strong king and good fortune might see a period, as with Oengus to come, when his rule extended over the entire territory of the Picts. Vigorous local leaders and internecine disputes could also bring times when the kingdom was virtually fragmented into its provinces. On the whole, the northern tribes had shown an ability to combine, especially in emergency, from the days of Calgacus onwards. By the early seventh century, their world looked less stable than it had 100 years before. The Scots were, by now, a substantial people – the evidence of the *Senchus Fer nAlban* suggests they were subdivided, in islands and mainland, into seven major groups – and Pictland was the natural place for them to expand into. The Angles of Northumbria, with a terrifying record of success in warfare, were on the southern frontier. Strathclyde was shrunken and on the defensive. But if the balance of power was changing, Pictland remained strong.

The Divisions of Pictland

Internally, it was divided into provinces or subkingdoms. Traditionally, these are taken to be seven in number. In (Scottish) legend the first king of the Picts is Cruithne (the name corresponds to Old Welsh *Priteni* and simply means 'inhabitant of Britain'). He had seven sons among whom the kingdom was distributed, and their names were given to their own domains: Fib, Fidach, Foltlaig, Fortrenn, Caitt, Ce, and Circinn. It is important to bear in mind that there is no direct Pictish source of information for any of this; we have tenuous Scots-Gaelic sources only, as previously noted. Some of these names can be matched up with territorial names that are found in other early documents:

Fib corresponds to *Fife*.

Fortrenn corresponds to *Fortriu* (from Verturiones), a tribal name identified with Strathearn.

Foltlaig corresponds to *Atholl*.

Caitt corresponds to *Caithness*, and included eastern Sutherland also.

Circinn has no present-day form; we know it refers to Angus.

Ce has no present-day form; it is taken to refer to part of the Aberdeenshire-Banffshire area.

Fidach has no present-day form; it is usually taken to refer to the Moray-Nairn-Inverness area. Its apparent resemblance to Fiddich has not been confirmed by place-name specialists.

None of these names appears to cover the substantial district of Ross, nor the farther northwest and Hebrides. Caitt may have included the northern islands; Shetland was known in Gaelic as *Innse Catt*. This name, like some of the older tribal names recorded by Ptolemy, has been taken as a totemic one: that of the 'cat people'. One name at least, Foltlaig, the genitive of Fotla, is Gaelic. The others are assumed to be Pictish in origin. A later document, dating from the twelfth century, *De Situ Albanie*, 'Of the Composition of Alba', lists a slightly different septet:

Enegus with Moerne (Angus and the Mearns). *Circinn*.
Adtheodle with Gouerin (Atholl and Gowrie). *Foltlaig*.

Sradeern with Meneted (Strathearn and Menteith). *Fortriu*.
Fif with Fothreve (Fife with Fothreve). *Fib*.
Marr with Buchen (Mar and Buchan). *Ce*.
Muref with Ros (Moray and Ross).
Cathanesia (divided into two, one on each side of the
    Mound (Ord). *Caitt*.

The later names correspond to the medieval divisions of
Caledonia. The paired names suggest the associated rule of a king
and of a subking. Their etymology is of great interest, though
sometimes controversial or impenetrable. Fothreve preserves the
Cumbric word *tref*, still found in Welsh as 'town', and the prefix
vo, 'lesser', 'subordinate', in a Gaelicised form, and refers to the
area around Kinross. *De Situ Albanie* also indicates, from twelfth-
century records, which may, of course, have originated far earlier
(much of the area in the twelfth century was under Norse control), approximate boundaries for five of these seven provinces,
which helps to confirm their geographical positions.

  Most of these provinces survived to become earldoms in the
medieval Scottish kingdom. But we lack information on the
composition of provinces in seventh- and eighth-century
Pictland, and on the relationship between provincial kings and
the king of Picts on the one hand, and between provincial
kings and their own subordinate chiefs on the other. From the
discrepancies between the lists we do possess, it is likely that
boundaries were liable to change and possible that whole
provinces merged or demerged at times.

The Threat from Northumbria

Aedan, king of Scots, died in 606, to be succeeded by his son
Eochaidh Buidhe, 'the yellow-haired'. The seventh-century
record of kings is very uncertain both for Scots and for Picts. It
may have been problematic for record-keepers at the time.
One historian has written:

' . . . from the time of Eochaidh Buidhe, right on till the reign of Kenneth MacAlpin, the kingdom only at intervals existed as an organic whole.' (Mitchell, 91)

The kingdom referred to is that of the Scots. From the bare record, it is impossible to say whether a king named in the list had authority over all the people, or whether he was simply the head of the Cineal Gabhràn or Comgall, still the most prestigious groups. There was warfare between different factions in the reign of Eochaidh, and he appears to have withdrawn from or been forced out of the kingship by his nephew Ferchar. There is an intriguing but unsupported reference in the 'Annals of Ulster' to the fact that Eochaidh ended his days as 'king of the Picts' (M. Anderson, 151). His name does not figure in the Pictish king list, though, as a royal refugee in Pictland (if he were such), he might have been installed as a Pictish provincial subking, possibly in Gowrie. A local warlord from Kintyre, Conadh Cerr, 'dark-haired', appears to have made a bid for overall power, to be defeated at the battle of Faedhaeoin, an unknown site, in 629.

From 629, the king of Scots was Domnall Breacc, 'speckled' or 'mottled'. In a battle recorded as having taken place in Glen Mairison in 638, Domnall was defeated, presumably by Picts, if the name corresponds to that of Glen Moriston. Such a site would suggest renewed attempts at incursions from Dàl Riada up the Great Glen. It has also been suggested that it was a battle against the Northumbrians, fought somewhere in West Lothian. Dissension among the Scots had spilled back into their old homeland of Ulster, and Domnall suffered a crushing defeat there at Moira in 639. A warlike but unsuccessful king, he seems to have been bereft of policy and to have fought with everyone. In 643, he was killed fighting the Britons under their king Owen in Strathcarron (the Stirling Carron), his end celebrated in these triumphant lines inserted into the *Gododdin*:

'I saw the array that came from Pentir (Kintyre)
It was as victims for the sacrifice they came down . . .
I saw the men beaten or wounded who came with the dawn,
And the head of Dyvnwal Vrych ravens gnawed it.'

This anachronistic interpolation of a Strathclyde victory into
one of the surviving texts of the *Gododdin* poem has been
explained as a complimentary addition made by a bard, who
sang the *Gododdin* to the court of king Owen at Dumbarton.
The Britons consequently gained territory at the Scots'
expense, perhaps for a time right up as far as Dunadd in the
Dàl Riadan heartland. But whatever clashes went on among
the northern Celtic kingdoms were to be dwarfed in significance by the mid-century onslaught of the Northumbrians.

Aedan's failed campaign against the Northumbrians in 603
may have been intended as a pre-emptive move in anticipation
of further Anglian advances. These duly materialised, though
delayed by struggles over the Northumbrian kingship. In 617,
the sons of Aethelfrith had been exiled by the new king,
Edwin of Deira. At least one of them, Eanfrith, took refuge
with the Picts, where he made a royal marriage; his son
Talorcan would become the king of the Picts between 653 and
657. Eanfrith returned to rule Bernicia briefly during a temporary break-up of Northumbria into its two old components
but the saintly, though warlike, king Oswald restored unity in
633. A victory by Talorcan over the Scots is noted in 654.
Talorcan's kingship has been used to support the arguments of
those who believe that the Picts practised matrilinear succession, but it has also been suggested that he was a puppet king
installed by Northumbrian power. Dr A. P. Smyth says:

'It makes at least as much sense to accept that Talorgen's accession to the Pictish kingship in 653 was part of Oswiu's policy
of expansion and domination in northern Britain, as it does to
hold that it came about by a matrilinear system of succession.'

Oswiu was Oswald's brother and successor but, in 653, his campaign had not begun, and it is hard to see how he was in a position to impose a king on the Picts. A few years later, possibly after Talorcan had been succeeded by another Gartnait in 657, the Northumbrians, under Oswiu, succeeded in establishing their control over the whole area between the Tay and and the Tweed, including the kingdom of the Scots. The Strathclyde Britons and the Scots were put under tribute, and southern Pictland was occupied. How large this occupied zone was is not clear. It almost certainly included Fife, and may have extended as far as Angus, thus claiming Pictish royal centres like Forteviot and Abernethy. The kings of Strathclyde and of Scots were reduced to tributary status. Dr Smyth reminds us that both Oswiu and Oswald, also sons of Aethelfrith, had been made welcome on Iona during their time of exile; they kept up cultural and religious links with the Scots, and their control of Lothian meant an incursion of Gaelic Church influence as well as of Northumbrian government – and maybe art styles (Smyth, 31).

In Pictland, Gartnait appears to have withdrawn beyond the Mounth into the northern provinces. He may have had family links with Skye, and Dr Isabel Henderson takes him as the Gartnait recorded in the 'Annals of Ulster', whose sons fled to Ireland 'with the people of Skye' ('North Pictland' from Meldrum, *The Dark Ages in the Highlands*). For 30 years, the Northumbrian hegemony continued. It is possible that the leaders of the Britons were acting as allies or agents of the Northumbrians at this time, against the recalcitrant Scots and the only partly-conquered Picts. The kings of this age are no more than names, but it seems that hostilities in Argyll continued between different members of the Cineal Gabhrain who fought one another for the kingship until, for the first time, in 676, a scion of the Cineal Loairn was able to oust the titular king, Maelduin, and establish himself, Ferchar Fada,'tall', as king of the stress-ridden Dàl Riata. He was able to focus on external problems, to some extent. In 678, he lost a battle against the Britons and, in 683, he was attempting to recapture Dunadd from them.

The Pictish Kingship

The kingship of Talorcan brings up the still-disputed issue of how the Picts chose their kings. As the history has already shown, the kingship of the Picts was a far from static institution. We have seen it move from Inverness to Angus, before apparently centring in the province or subkingdom of Fortriu. Some scholars have seen it as a centralised kingship and referred to a 'Pictish state'; others have been equally sure that there was no continuous centrally-ruled Pictish state and that only occasional strong figures like the two Brideis, macBile and macDerilei, and Oengus, were able to assert themselves over all or most of the lands inhabited by Picts. Such overlordships are thus seen as personal and transient, rather than as part of a political continuum. Following the southward move of the kings, distinctions have been made between 'northern' and 'southern' Picts, separated by the Mounth, with Moray, and the coastland stretching round the head of the Cromarty Firth, as the northerners' main zone of population, and the southerners concentrated in Angus, Strathearn, and Fife. No 'capital' has been recognised in the northern region at this time, though there is no lack of fortified sites, including that at Burghead with its famous underground well, as well as king Bridei's one-time stronghold at or close by Inverness. But we really know practically nothing about how society north or south of the Mounth was administered at this time, and even less about the area north of the Great Glen, and the northern isles. It is not known why the kings should have moved from the central location of Inverness to the southern fringes of Pictish territory. There is far more information about the Angus-Atholl-Strathearn region, which, along its western edge, bordered with Dàl

Riada, than there is about the north. Statements made with regard to this southern Pictland should not be interpreted as being valid for the north, in this or any other book.

The means by which Pictish kings acceded to power are still contested. Marjorie Anderson, the most diligent researcher into the matter, was certain (in 1973) that the kingship was inherited by matrilineal succession; that is, by virtue of the candidate's mother being what she was, namely a queen or princess of Pictish royal blood. This does not discount the father's status, but it does not make it essential for him to have been a Pict. He could be a member of a royal line from any other kingdom. This practice – exogamy – was frequent among the rulers of the kingdoms of Britain, as it was among royal families in other countries, though usually by the import of a wife rather than a husband. In its strictest form, exogamy forbade marriage within the tribe. Such marriages did not apparently imply a permanent liaison: having fulfilled his function of siring a royal child, the husband might return to his own people. In this context, we are reminded of the role of women in some other, earlier Celtic societies – reigning queens like Boudicca and Cartimandua in south Britain. From north Britain, there are the proud words of the wife of a Caledonian leader to Julia Domna, Septimius Severus's empress, recorded by Dio in 210 during the Severan campaign in Caledonia: 'We have intercourse openly with the best of men.' This almost suggests polyandry. As a matter of record, the sole existing Pictish king list that has survived (in differing copies) lists each king as the son of his father. His paternity was thus known and considered significant, even though none of these fathers were themselves kings of the Picts. The mothers' names are not recorded in the list. The king list itself is only regarded as trustworthy from the mid-sixth century. Anderson's view is maintained by professor A. A. M. Duncan in *Scotland: Making of the Kingdom*, but the 'matrilineal tradition' is stoutly challenged and relegated to the status of 'myth' by A. P. Smyth in *Warlords and Holy Men*.

The argument is an important one, since succession through the mother rather than the father would be a tradition unique in western Europe, and opens the door to other ways in which the Picts might be seen as heirs of a completely different tradition to that of their neighbours, and possibly a more ancient one. Writers on European prehistory have noted that the Mediterranean peoples were originally matrilinear, and worshipped the earth goddess, while the Indo-Europeans were patrilinear and had a masculine-dominated pantheon. Evidence for the Pictish matrilinear tradition starts with Bede, who was writing shortly before 730, when the Pictish kingdom was still a going concern, and we have already noted his retelling of an Irish legend to the effect that the wifeless Picts originally obtained their womenfolk from the inhabitants of Ireland, on condition that 'when any dispute arose, they should choose a king from the female royal line rather than the male. This custom continues among the Picts to this day' (Bede, 1,i).

Smyth investigates the matrilineal case and is able to show that none of the evidence for the system is conclusive. Keen to demystify the Picts, to close the door on mother goddesses and other speculative, and frequently wild, theories, and to show that they were, in all essentials, a typical Celtic people, he then presents his own case for 'normal' patrilineal succession. It is well constructed but rests sufficiently on supposition for the matter not to be solidly proven. An important element in his argument is his claim that the two most famous kings issuing from 'exogamic' marriages – Talorcan, son of the Anglian refugee, Eanfrith, and Bridei macBili, the victor of Nechtansmere – were both imposed from outside: Talorcan by king Oswiu of Northumberland, whose supremacy over the southern Picts is well attested; and Bridei by the Strathclyde Britons. In Bridei's case, he even queries whether there was a Pictish mother, but his key point is that *Machtpolitik*, and not matriliny, got them their crowns. Neither case is entirely convincing. Talorcan's kingship appears to predate Oswiu's conquest, as has been already noted. In the case of Bridei, Dr Smyth believes, by means of a distinctly speculative hypothesis, that the Strathclyde Britons held the overkingship of the Picts at this time. But, at that time, Strathclyde itself was under the overlordship of Northumbria, as Bede makes clear, while Pictland, though partly occupied, was not. It seems unlikely that, in such a situation, Strathclyde could have imposed itself enough on the still-independent Picts to provide them with a king whom they did not want.

Although Dr Smyth leaves the arguments for the matrilineal succession severely battered, the lack of conclusive evidence either way has left the matter still unresolved and, like a pair of ironclads unable to pierce each other's armour plate, both arguments remain leakily but obstinately afloat. Smyth is rightly hostile to the element of wishful thinking in Pictish studies, in which the desire for the Picts to be 'different' can obscure the extent to which they, in many respects, share the same practices, customs, and beliefs as their neighbours.

The Greatest Victory

In Pictland, Oswiu used his kinship with his nephew Talorcan to claim that the Pictish kingship should devolve upon himself, and thus to legitimise his occupation of the south. A Pictish king, Drest, appears to have been installed from around 665; if this was in the south, it can only have been as a puppet ruler under Northumbrian control. Oswiu died in 670 or 671, and soon after that, in 672, there was an uprising among the Picts, in which Drest was ousted. It may be the case that Drest, who was a northerner, brother to Gartnait, was the leader of this uprising and was ousted by the Northumbrians, rather than by his own people. In any case, the revolt was savagely put down by the occupying power. The new Northumbrian king, Ecgfrith, urged on by his sainted bishop Wilfred, is said to have heaped Pictish corpses across two rivers to enable his army to cross dry-shod. While this detail, admiringly recorded by Wilfred's biographer, Eddius Stephanus, is a stock phrase, it is a stock phrase that indicates bloody reprisal and massacre.

Following this disaster, and the reinforcement of Northumbrian control in the south, a new king of the Picts, Bridei macBile, emerges in somewhat obscure fashion. Bridei was a typical product of royal intermarriage, related to the Strathclyde rulers through his father Bile. His brother, or half-brother, was Owen, the vigorous king of Strathclyde who had defeated Domnall Breacc of the Scots. On his mother's side, he has been assumed to be Pictish, though it has been pointed out that there is no clear evidence of this. On the other hand, there is nothing to suggest why or how someone of no Pictish parentage at all could assume the kingship at such a critical moment. He is supposed by some historians to be a grandson of Eanfrith through his mother (assumed to be Talorcan's sister), and so in this way eligible for the kingship. As a mention in the *Historia Brittonum* points out, he was also then a cousin to his opponent Ecgfrith. His election – if a choice was involved – amply justified the confidence of the Pictish elders.

Bridei first established himself, not in the south of Pictland – the occupied territory – but in the still-independent north. The sparse details of his campaigns shed elusive glimmerings of light on the situation among the northern Picts. A siege of Dunottar in 681 is recorded, which must have involved Picts either as attackers or defenders; though Bridei's name is not noted in connection with it, neither is anyone else's. He made what seems to have been a punitive expedition to Orkney in 682, causing great destruction. A siege of a place referred to as Dunbaitte is also recorded; this was taken by W. F. Skene to be Dunbeath on the coast of Caithness (Skene, i, 263), which suggests attempts at local independence in the far north, perhaps associated with events in Orkney. At the same time as Ferchar Fada's attempt to recapture Dunadd, Bridei, by coincidence or concerted design, was besieging the Britons who were at that time also in possession of Dundurn, the strategic rock fort in Strathfillan, in southwest Pictland. Such an action does not suggest any strong bond between himself and his brother Owen.

Bridei's move southwards brought Ecgfrith of Northumbria into action. In the early summer of 685, he marched north with his army to re-establish the Northumbrian hold on southern Pictland. Bridei retreated tactically before him, to a site recorded by the English as Nechtansmere and by the Gaels as Duin Nechtain, generally accepted to be in the vicinity of Dunnichen in Angus, where there was, until the 18th century, a small loch known as the Mire of Dunnichen. On 20 May, in this hummocky green countryside, where the Sidlaws slope down towards Strathmore, the Picts won their greatest victory, great both in its scale and in its significance. Indeed, its importance to the independence of Scotland would not be matched until Bruce's victory at Bannockburn 600 years later. Only sketchy details of the battle are recorded, but the Northumbrian army was apparently lured into a classic trap. The Picts feigned a retreat into the hills and, in pursuing, it was attacked by Bridei's main force, lying in ambush, overwhelmed, and destroyed. Ecgfrith was killed; his body sent by the victors to Iona for honourable burial. A victory for Ecgfrith could have brought the whole of Pictland under Anglian hegemony, in which case the prospect of an independent nation, whether Pictish or Scottish in its constitution, would have been very doubtful. After Dunnichen, the Northumbrian bid for empire was finished. Bridei was master of Pictland, and of the overall situation north and west of the Forth. Bede wrote:

' ...the Picts recovered the territory belonging to them which the Angles had held, and the Scots who were in Britain, and a certain part of the Britons, regained their liberty . . . ' (Bede, iv, 26)

Thanks to the Pictish victory, Scots and Strathclyde Britons ceased paying tribute to the Angles. The latter retained possession of Lothian, under the charge of an *ealdorman*, or earl, based at Dunbar. During their ascendancy, they had established a bishopric at Abercorn on the south shore of the Firth of Forth, in 681. Headed by an Anglian cleric, Trumwine, this was intended as the bishopric of the Picts, replacing the autonomous Church structure that had developed in Pictland. It may say something about the strength of the Northumbrian grip on southern Pictland that they could not apparently set up Trumwine's Church in Abernethy, or any other established holy site within the Pictish kingdom. In 685, following the battle at Dunnichen, the bishopric collapsed and Trumwine returned to Whitby Abbey in Northumbria.

In Galloway, the ancient foundation at Whithorn had been brought into the Anglian scheme of things, and made subject to the bishop of Durham; the position after 685 is less clear, though Sir Frank Stenton believed that

' . . . it is improbable that Galloway or any part of the Solway coast was in their [Strathclyde] hands. Within fifty years of Ecgfrith's death, Whithorn, the most famous church of Galloway, had become the seat of an English bishopric, and one of the greatest of Northumbrian crosses had been erected at Ruthwell near Dumfries.' (Stenton)

The Strathclyde Britons played no part at Nechtansmere, and the new Pictish ascendancy is likely to have pushed them back inside their old frontiers, leaving the southern fringe of Galloway under strong Northumbrian influence and perhaps actual control.

CHAPTER FOUR

The Picts' Great Century

Pictish Life

'What I like about Pictish studies is that they have made
so little headway. Here is a large, artistically gifted nation,
that was famous in Europe for 800 years, and yet we
know less about it than eighteenth-century cockneys
knew about Central Africa.'

Neal Ascherson, *Games with Shadows* (1988)

'No other country in northern Europe, except perhaps Ireland,
is so rich in visible relics of the ancient world,' wrote the historian H. M. Chadwick of Scotland in 1949; he took the sanguine
view that there was much Pictish material to be interpreted,
and since his time many more sites and relics have been
explored or identified. Other writers have felt that there was
little enough material, and its message was often obscure.

While the written record is scanty, and consists almost wholly
of texts written outside Scotland, the record of the stones is substantial and very much on the spot. In the past, this sometimes
made for uneasy relations between historians and archaeologists,
before it became clear that a combined approach was much more
likely to produce a coherent and increasingly detailed and accurate picture of life and culture in the first millennium CE.

Comments by classical writers, and suppositious illustrations of Picts like those made by the English 16th-century artist-explorer, John White, once led to the notion that the Picts went habitually naked, in order perhaps to display their tattooed bodies. Even given a milder climate, this might seem improbable (though the Yaghan people at a comparable southern latitude at the chilly extreme tip of South America were still naked in the 19th century. But they were in a much more primitive condition than the Picts). The evidence of their carved stones makes it clear that the Picts, by the eighth century anyway, wore a variety of warm garments. Only two pieces of clothing, apart from buttons and pins, from this long period have been recovered: a woman's fringed shawl and headdress, woven from wool, found in peat at St Andrew's, Orkney; and a fine decorated soft leather shoe, dated to the seventh or eighth century, from Dundurn, in western Perthshire.

The detailed scenes often found on Class II sculptured stones are of value in providing information. As the antiquary Joseph Anderson, wrote in 1881:

' . . . we learn from a comparison of all the different representations that the horsemen of that period rode without spurs or stirrups, cropped the manes and tails of their horses, used snaffle-bridles with check rings and ornamental rosettes, and sat upon peaked saddle-cloths; that, when journeying on horseback, they wore peaked hoods and cloaks, and when hunting or on horseback, armed, they wore a kilt-like dress, falling below mid-thighs, and a plaid across the shoulders; that they used long-bows in war, and cross-bows in hunting, that their swords were long, broad-bladed, double-edged, obtusely pointed weapons with triangular pommels and straight guards; that their spears had large, lozenge-shaped heads, while their bucklers were round and furnished with bosses; that when journeying on foot they wore trews or tight-fitting nether garments, and a plaid loosely-wrapped around the body, or a tight jerkin with sleeves, and belt round the waist; that they wore their hair long, flowing, and curly, sometimes with peaked beards, at other times with moustaches on the upper lip and shaven cheeks and chin; that they used covered chariots or two-wheeled carriages with poles for draught by two horses, the driver sitting on a seat over the pole, the wheels having ornamental spokes; that they used chairs with side-arms and high, curved backs, sometimes ornamented with heads of animals; that their boats had high prows and stern-posts; that the long dresses of the ecclesiastics were richly embroidered; that they walked in loose short boots, and carried crosiers and book-satchels.' (*Scotland in Early Christian Times*)

A modern writer might avoid the use of the words 'kilt' and 'plaid', which interpret the carvings rather too much in terms of later costume, and could be taken to imply a continuity of the Pictish costume into the Highland dress of medieval and later periods: something that cannot be proved. It is in fact little enough information, from the whole life of a people, but it is much more than can be obtained from any other European source in the eighth and ninth centuries.

Among the somewhat enigmatic artefacts we have that go back to Pictish times are twelve silver chains, made of double links, two of which have terminal links engraved with Pictish symbols. The chains have come from various sites between Inverness and Lothian. Seven were found south of Pictland – one, from Whitecleugh in Lanarkshire, being one of the two with Pictish motifs – and this has led to the supposition that they were removed as plunder during the Northumbrian occupation of southern Pictland in the seventh century. It is assumed that these chains were tokens of kingship. Gold might have been expected as symbolic of regality but, surprisingly, no gold items are associated with the Picts.

Representations of instruments of several types attest to the presence of music in people's lives. The later carved stones, from the ninth and tenth centuries, often display the harp, both as a large and as a portable instrument (the latter perhaps a precursor of the Highland clarsach). While the sculptural context is a Biblical one, with David often the harpist, the instrument is clearly depicted from knowledge. The other instruments, blast horns and (from the first and second centuries) the animal-headed carnyx, or war horn, suggest ceremonial and military uses. Evidence of board games has been found at a number of sites, such as peg figures at Clatchard Craig in Fife, an engraved board at Dun Chanalaich in Argyll, and gaming counters at the Buchlyvie 'Fairy Knowe'. Later Irish stories often mention chess, but it is unlikely that chess was played in Scotland before the ninth century.

Numerous Pictish stones display hunting scenes. In some cases, these have been given a spiritual or mystic significance by observers: the 'holy hunt', in which Christ pursues the sinner in order to overcome and redeem him. Their detail suggests a more secular purpose too, and they may possibly praise the prowess and sanctity of a particular king or queen, in the manner of Renaissance patrons having themselves depicted in association with the Holy Family. Whatever the ultimate motive, here too there is a veracity of detail, a precision of pose and movement, a pride in weaponry, showing clearly that horseback hunting itself was an integral and highly esteemed aspect of life. It is very much the pleasure of 'the chase' rather than a necessity for survival that is being depicted. The Picts are much nearer to us than they are to the doughty spearmen of the Lascaux cave paintings.

The only representation of a Pictish ship is found on a ninth-century carving known as St Orland's stone, from Cossans Farm, in Angus. Much of the detail is worn away, but it shows a double-ended boat, manned by ten oarsmen, with a built-up stem, no mast, and a steering oar. The hull could be of wood or hide, but the latter is more likely. In post-Roman times, the Picts retained a substantial fleet. The 'Annals of

Tigernach' for 729 record that 150 Pictish ships were wrecked off a point called Ros Cuissini, identified as Troup Head in Buchan (where Cushnie remains as a nearby inland name). Even if the vessels were small, it was a disaster notable enough to be recorded. The fleet has been supposed to be involved in the war for the kingship between Nechtan (who traditionally is associated with northern Pictland) and Oengus, though it may have been fishing boats on the track of a shoal of herring. The Ros Cuissini disaster comes 20 years after a battle against the Orkneys in 709 and, prior to that, there had been an invasion of these islands by king Bridei in 683. H. M. Chadwick suggests that the attacks noted on the Pictish fortress of Dunottar in 681 and 694 may have been made by fleets coming down from Orkney. Again the unruly state of Orkney is evident, though the existence of seventh- and eighth-century Pictish symbol stones in both Orkney and Shetland, and other evidence of Pictish art, suggest that by that time, if not before, the islands had been brought into the Pictish cultural area.

The humble activity of tilling the soil is not represented in the upper-class imagery of the Pictish carvings. Long before the coming of the Romans, agriculture had become established among the tribes as a mixture of arable and pastoral activity; and farming was the prime concern of all these communities. Each group had to be self-sufficient, and that meant producing enough food in the growing season to last through the winter. For coastal communities, and few were far from the coast, and even then were usually by a river or loch, there was also the harvest of the waters. The diet of the tribes appears to have been a varied one, as far as can be ascertained from the middens they left. Fish, shellfish, birds, birds' eggs, deer and seal meat were all eaten. The inhabitants of Scotland between around 100 and 1000CE enjoyed a more varied and sustaining diet than did the great majority of their descendants in the 18th and early 19th centuries, although there must have been many times of near or actual starvation when a hard winter was followed by a late spring.

Hunting, stalking, and fishing were all of great importance. The domesticated animals were cows, horses, sheep, goats, and pigs. Adamnan's *Life of St Columba*, in its incidental details of abbey life on Iona, confirms the use of horses as draught animals. Perhaps wild cattle and ponies roamed the hills in the early centuries CE. The tradition that the cattle 'belonged to no one' died hard in the Highlands, though it may simply have been a means of giving licence to the time-honoured practice of the cattle raid. An important aspect of 'fortification' was simply to keep animals penned in, safe from raiders or wolves. Beef formed a large part of the diet, more than half of it in the remains that have been found (Foster). Nothing was wasted. Animals that reached the end of their working lives, or died of disease, were eaten, their hides flayed off for leatherware or parchment. Only the unusable bones went to the dump.

The communities also made use of a great many plants now neglected. Nettles were used as a source of cloth-making flax in Scotland up to the 18th century. Excavators in the damp lower levels of the Dundurn fort found evidence of sphagnum moss used as the equivalent of toilet paper. Wild-growing herbs, nuts, fungi, fruit, and berries were also picked in season and used for food and in medicines. Bees were kept and the honey and beeswax put to use. To supplement the universally available water and milk, ale and mead were made. Part of the cereal crop presumably went to the brewing of ale, though the Picts in ancient legend also had the secret of heather ale.

How numerous the population was during the first millennium is difficult to gauge. But there is a trend for all estimates of early population to be revised upwards in the light of new archaeological discoveries. Tacitus had estimated the Caledonian army at 30,000 in 83CE. This might imply a population of around ten times that in the catchment area of the fighters. About 700 years later, the *Senchus fer nAlban*, in its second assessment, though hard to make a count from, would put the strength of the tribes of the Dàl Riata at around 3200 warriors, plus those who would man galleys. If 1500 men went on sea service, on the same basis as before, this would suggest a population of about 47,000 for Argyll and the adjacent islands, including Mull and Islay. Any figures for Picts, Britons, and Angles at the beginning of the eighth century are pure guesswork. But it would seem possible that, with a large margin for error, as many as 500,000 people shared the natural resources of the land during the eighth century (the first fairly scientific census of Scotland, in 1756, established a population then of about 1,500,000).

The inhabitants were more evenly distributed than the population of present-day Scotland. Each community required both cultivable ground and pastureland, including high summer pasture. In addition, it needed access to the resources of forest and water. This does not imply a free-for-all situation; most, if not all, resources were specially designated or reserved. Many place names show the importance attached to defining land areas and boundaries. Adamnan notes that seal-trapping rights off part of the island of Mull were reserved to the monks of Iona (abbot Columcille had to deal with a poacher on at least one occasion), and it can be fairly assumed, despite the lack of charters or other evidence, that all productive zones of land and sea were carefully noted and subdivided, and rights to these subdivisions assigned or confirmed through the king or chief. Transgression of these rights would be a serious offence. Perhaps only the high slopes and plateaux, and thickest forest, where the deer and wild boar roamed without regard to human boundaries, might be unallocated – or more probably reserved to royalty.

A King with Ideas

Bridei, king of the Picts, died in 693, after what appear to have been some peaceful years, and Adamnan notes his burial on Iona. Another death recorded around the same time is that of Tuathal, first recorded bishop of Fothrife, and also abbot of Dunkeld; one of the few indications from this time of the organised Pictish Church. Bridei's successor, Taran, was deposed after four years by Bridei macDerelei. Early in the latter's reign, a battle against the Anglians is recorded, in which their leader was killed. In 706, Bridei died, and another son of Derelei, Nechtan, assumed the kingship. Once again there was war with the Anglians early in the reign, and this time (711) the Picts were beaten by an army under the ealdorman of Dunbar, though without any recorded consequence. These may have been little more than border skirmishes, but if they were more serious, they may have been part of the reason for Nechtan's great diplomatic initiative. He embarked on a new external policy by establishing friendly relations with the Northumbrians. Themselves under pressure in the south from the recently-grown power of Mercia, they may have needed him more than he needed them. A Pictish-Northumbrian entente was not good news for the Scots and Britons, especially the latter, who now saw the two greatest powers on their borders in alliance. Up till now, from the evidence available, it has been hard to see the kings as other than war leaders, since battles are almost the only recorded details of their actions. Nechtan's reign shows that a king could have a programme of action in other areas. An overture was made by the Pictish king to the Northumbrian Church, to assist the Pictish Church in the reform of its observances.

Kings and priests worked closely together. The spiritual mantle of the priest-king still had meaning, and there was no separation of the sacred and the secular aspects of life. Senior clerics played a part in the government of the kingdom, both through their own positions and, very often, as members of ruling families. The Church was a significant part of the power structure of the kingdom, and not easily separable from the time-honoured kinship-based authority of the king and his close kindred, whose adherence to the Church's faith and teachings contributed to the Church's prestige.

The evidence of Pictish art speaks for a spiritual quality among the people. Matters of religious practice and national policy were as inextricably linked in the eighth century as they were 900 years later, in the Scotland of the 17th century. For Pictland until now, the accepted headquarters of religious teaching and practice had been Iona. Pictish kings were taken to the island for burial. Just before Nechtan's time, Iona had also had its most influential and distinguished abbot since Columcille himself – the saint's biographer, Adamnan.

Despite Iona's pre-eminence – always greater when viewed from Scotland rather than from Ireland – the Irish Church remained a federation, rather than a hierarchy on the Roman model. In exile, Oswald son of Aethelfrith had lived on Iona. When he became king of Northumbria in 633, he sent to the island for a bishop to come and teach Christianity to the pagan Angles. The Northumbrian Church, from its first base on Lindisfarne, was established on the Celtic model by its first bishop, St Aidan, sent from Iona. But, by the middle of the seventh century, it had shaken off its Celtic aspects and conformed to the rule and doctrines of Rome, as expounded by the papally appointed incumbents of the recently established bishopric of Canterbury. Northumbria's up-and-coming clerics, like the redoubtable Wilfred, were by then Anglians, not Scots. At the Synod of Whitby in 664, called by king Oswiu of Northumbria, Wilfred had won the debate with the Ionan bishop Colman over the central issues of the dating of Easter and the form of a monk's tonsure. To a secular age, these seem minor matters, but the Celtic churchmen, with a long tradition not merely of independence, but of maintaining the faith when it had all but collapsed elsewhere, saw the abandonment of these practices as a rejection of 200 years of devoted labour. It was a further source of gall that the changes were being promoted by their erstwhile daughter Church in Northumbria. A vital aspect of the society both of Scots and Picts, inseparable from the mores of a warrior-led aristocracy, was a passion for prestige. Christian humility notwithstanding, the priests also shared this thin-skinned prickly sense of pride and honour.

Bede relates that the first bishop of Canterbury, pope Gregory's emissary, St Augustine, offended clerics from the Churches already established in Britain, when he refused to rise from his chair to greet them on their arrival at a meeting. Such things were far from being considered trivial, and Wilfred's clever sneer, borrowed from the headquarters briefing of a Lateran missive, was both insulting and wounding:

> 'The only people who are stupid enough to disagree with the whole world are these Scots and their obstinate adherents the Picts and the Britons, who inhabit only a portion of these two islands in the remote ocean.' (Bede, iii, 25)

(He appears, incidentally, to have been the first person to identify and patronise what much later was called 'the Celtic fringe'.) It was a bitter pill for the monks of Iona to admit to their own people that they, and the great Columba before them, had been practising a flawed rite. Even though their abbot, Adamnan, who died in 704, accepted the Roman view, his own community continued to reject it until at least 716.

The controversy caused serious divisions in the Church between those who resisted conformity with Rome and those who accepted it. It is against this background of intense dispute that the activities of king Nechtan must be considered. In 710, following a convocation of his own advisers, he decreed that, in Pictland, the Roman rule would be followed. To achieve this, he sent for guidance on correct practice to Ceolfrith, abbot of Jarrow, at the mouth of the Northumbrian Tyne. He also asked Ceolfrith 'that architects be sent to him in order to build a stone church for his people in the proper Roman style'. The abbot supplied the necessary information in a lengthy and detailed letter and, it is assumed, master masons duly turned up to undertake the royal commission.

To implement the new practice, the consent of the clergy was necessary. It is not clear whether this was obtained. Bede states that Iona accepted Catholic practice in 716, though other sources suggest that dissension continued within the Celtic Church through the eighth century. But, in 717, it is recorded that the Columban clergy were expelled from Pictland. This drastic action may have been because they refused to conform to the Roman rule, or because they were quarrelling among themselves. Another motive has been inferred by some modern writers. Their premise is that the language of the Church, when it was not Latin, was Gaelic. The monks themselves, mostly emerging from the schools of Iona, or Bangor in Ireland, were Gaelic in their speech and Scots in their allegiance. In expelling them, Nechtan was taking deliberate action to preserve the Pictish language and the Pictish state against a 'Scotticising' tendency (we have seen how St Wilfred referred to the Picts as 'adherents' of the Scots). There is no evidence for or against this suggestion. Abbots such as Adamnan seem to have taken pains to preserve Iona's status as a supranational institution, which served many kingdoms, and to maintain the independence that allowed it to intercede or arbitrate without being accused of partiality, but the priests and monks of Pictland may have taken a more partisan line. The monastery at Applecross, on the northwest coast, established from Bangor by Maelrubha in 673, was in nominally Pictish territory, but it is likely that by then the whole west coast up to and including Applecross was in a Dàl Riadan area of influence, which came to be known as 'North Argyll'. We do not know what language was used in the Pictish Church; while Gaelic-Pictish bilingualism may have been common among the ruling families, it is not likely that the Pictish people in general had any cause to learn Gaelic. The reasons for Nechtan's action remain uncertain.

Drownings

There were signs of strain under Nechtan's rule. In 713, his brother, Ciniod, was killed by the subking of Atholl, who was

consequently imprisoned. Atholl was to remain a difficult
province. In 724, Nechtan entered a monastery, probably not
on a voluntary basis (in some accounts he is said to have
become a hermit, in a cave near Nigg, on the Moray Firth).
The Pictish kingship, having been stable since 685, was beginning to crumble, with a range of rival claimants appearing. For
four years, there was a confused period, with internecine battles recorded by the Irish annalists. Nechtan was replaced as
king by Drust, who made Nechtan a prisoner, but was himself
deposed in 726 and replaced by Alpin or Elpin macEachach. At
this time, an Eochach macEachach was king in Dàl Riada, and
these two may have been brothers. Family or tribal factions
were clearly at war. Another contestant was Oengus macFergus,
whose name strongly suggests Dàl Riatan ancestry on his
father's side. Oengus's forces attacked Alpin in 728 at a battle
recorded as *Monaigh Craebi*, 'hill of the trees', which has been
suggested as Moncrieffe, just south of Perth. Oengus was victor,
and established himself in the country to the west of the Tay.
Alpin was not eliminated, however, but in the same year
Nechtan, free again, also defeated him at a site called *Caislen
Credhi*, 'castle of belief', suggested as Scone. Alpin then disap-
pears into obscurity; Nechtan briefly resumed rule but, in 729,
Oengus met him in battle at Monith Carno, near Tyndrum, on
the marches of Pictland and Dàl Riada, and defeated him. The
naval disaster of that year at *Ros-Cuissini*, mentioned earlier, may
have been part of this campaign and a contribution to Nechtan's
downfall. Oengus then turned on Drust, who had rallied his
forces, and a battle was fought at an unknown ridge referred to
as *Druim Derg Blathuug*, on 12 August, 729. Drust was killed and
Oengus emerged as king, though his rule was still disputed until
731, when his son Brude defeated Talorcan macCongus, who
fled but was seized and judicially drowned three years later .
This form of execution seems to have been a frequent one
among the Picts and, despite the spread of Christianity, it had
sacrificial overtones. Ceremonial drowning was known to the

early Irish and continental tribes: one of the greatest items of first-century Celtic art, the silver cauldron found at Gundestrup in Denmark, shows a man about to be plunged head-first into a tank. The rock-cut basin, 1.2m (4ft) deep, at the important Pictish site of Burghead in Moray, though it may have become a Christian baptistery, was perhaps earlier a scene of such cult-related executions.

Warlords at Work

The travails of the Pictish monarchy were matched by those of the Scots. Around the end of the seventh century, the Cineal Loairn managed to take over the kingship of the Dàl Riata, in the person of Ferchar Fada, 'the tall', but, even within his own group, there was war over who should hold power. Ferchar Fada, having restored the integrity of the Dàl Riadan kingdom, ruled until 697. His latter years were troubled by the Cineal Gabhrain, under Eochaidh Rianamhail, 'hook nose', a grandson of Domhnall Breacc, until a rival in Eochaidh's own tribe assassinated him. Ferchar's son Ainbhcellach directly inherited the kingship, an unusual event in itself, but was driven out by Fiannamail of the Cineal Gabhrain. Fiannamail himself was killed in a different intertribal strife and the kingship was taken by Sealbach, Ainbhcellach's brother, in 698. 'Warlords' seems a fair expression for these individuals, whose memory is preserved only in records of battle and destruction. Sealbach's rule was marked by constant conflict, in which the fortress of Dunollie was destroyed three times in 14 years; he fought not only the Cineal Gabhrain, but also hostile elements in his own tribal group of Loairn. At least three battles with Strathclyde, a victory in *Valle Limnae*, probably the Vale of Leven in Dunbartonshire, in 704; a defeat at *Loirg eclat*, probably Loch Arklet, in 711; and another victory in 717 at *Minvircc*, identified with the site called *Clach nam Braetan*, 'stone of the Britons', in Glenfalloch, suggest that the territorial boundaries were still very much in dispute.

Two years later, Ainbhcellach led an invasion from Ireland in hopes of retrieving his position, but was killed in the battle of Findglen, close to Loch Avich, the site known in Gaelic as *Blar nan Brathrean*, 'field of the brothers'. Sealbach was however defeated in a sea battle in the same year against the Cineal Gabhrain, led by Duncadh, king of Kintyre. In 723, Sealbach retired to a monastery and his son Dungàl, 'the violent', assumed the kingship. Hostility to him within the Cineal Loairn resulted in his deposition in 726 and his uncle, Ewen or Heochgain, took his place. But it seems clear that there was no single rule, since Eochach macEachach is also recorded as being king from 726. A scion of the Cineal Gabhrain, he clung to power in his own region until his death in 733. Meanwhile, Sealbach renounced his improbable role as monk to come out and fight for his son, Dungàl. His support came from a district known as 'the two Airgiallas', identified by W. F. Skene as the lands on the eastern and western sides of Loch Awe. He made trouble until his death in 730, and Dungàl kept up a brigandish career after him.

These wars were fought on sea as well as on land. The *Senchus fer nAlban* makes clear that the rulers of Dàl Riada provided for the manning of a fleet as well as of a land army. Ships were necessary both to transport armed men and to repel the ships of aggressors. The earliest recorded sea battle in British waters was fought off the Argyll coast between the Cineal Loairn and the Cineal Gabhrain in 719, though there are references to ships used in warfare long before that. Although the first-century geographer, Strabo, says that the seafaring Veneti of northwest Gaul made boats of oak, the vessels of the northern tribes, as referred to by Gildas in the sixth century, are of the curragh type, made from waterproofed hides stretched and stitched over a framework of bentwood. This pattern could produce quite large boats, fitted with a mast and able to carry livestock and other cargo. But it was a relatively primitive form of shipbuilding, especially for peoples who had ample wood supply and sheltered building sites, and who had frequently seen wooden seagoing ships from the Mediterranean and Gaul during Roman times and afterwards. Here again is a sign of insular conservatism, this time among the shipwrights, and presumably caused by the obstinate fostering of their own hereditary practice. The obsolete nature of the Scots' shipping would be a severe disadvantage when the Norsemen, with far superior craft, began their raids and invasions.

After Eochach, the kingship remains with the Cineal Gabhrain, up to the appearance of Kenneth MacAlpin (who also claimed to be of that house). But as we have seen, the extent to which any overking of the Scots could exert authority over all the kindreds was extremely variable. The practice and the tradition by no means always matched each other. It is useful to remember that there was another aspect to the society of the Scots at this time. Artistic work of a high order was being accomplished at the monastery of Iona and perhaps at other abbeys. Iona's finest product, the *Book of Kells*, was probably not begun until later in the century, but it could not have been achieved without the existence of a confident and established artistic tradition in the abbey's scriptorium.

Pictish Supremacy

By 733, the warlike Oengus was in full and secure possession of the Pictish throne. The situation in Dàl Riada, by comparison, was still chaotic. Eochach died in 733. Ewen lived on until around 742, with authority among the Cineal Loairn. Alpin macEachach, having failed to become king of the Picts, may have succeeded Eochach until 737. A son of Ainbhcellach, Muredach, is recorded as king until 745, when he was succeeded by his son, Ewen. By then, however, Dàl Riada was a subject state of Pictland and its kings were tributaries to Oengus.

In 733, Oengus's son Brude, a war leader in his own right, was visiting the sanctuary on Tory Island, off the Irish coast, where the church had been founded by Columcille. Here he

was caught and taken prisoner by Dungàl. The seizing of
Brude provided Oengus with the reason or excuse to invade
Dàl Riada, a territory in which Dungàl had no overall control,
perhaps no real control at all. In the course of Oengus's attack,
a fortress called Dunleithfinn, an unknown site, was destroyed;
Dungàl was wounded, and fled to safety somewhere in Ireland.
Oengus captured the son of the king of Atholl, near Dunollie
(in 739, he was to have the king of Atholl drowned). In 736, he
again invaded the Scots in a much more wide-ranging attack, in
which he is said to have laid waste to the country. The campaign, in which Brude was killed, was not merely directed
against Dungàl. Oengus's brother defeated Muredach in an
unidentified area, Calathross, though the actual site, Etarlindu,
has been associated with Ederline by Loch Awe. Oengus had
not finished with Dàl Riada. In 741, he fought two further battles, possibly on Irish soil, to ensure his complete control of the
kingdom of the Scots.

It was the fragmentation of the tribal structure of Dàl Riada
that enabled Oengus I, having established himself in Pictland,
to invade and establish supremacy in the neighbouring kingdom in 734. On the face of it, this looks a different sort of
warfare – a campaign of Pictish imperialism, with Oengus
establishing Pictish laws in the conquered kingdom of the
Scots; it certainly goes far beyond being a border war. But,
although, as Marjorie Anderson points out, there is no entry in
the Annals to say that Oengus was a king of Dàl Riada, his
power base was in the politically ambiguous province of
Fortriu, and his decisive battle with Nechtan, at Monith
Carno, in 729, was fought right on the border of Pictland and
Dàl Riada (M. Anderson). Mrs Anderson, following the
matrilinear interpretation, suggests Oengus's father, Forgus,
may have been the son of a sister of Taran, the Pictish king
deposed around 696. Forgus's name is Irish, a form of Fergus
(though he is also found in the Pictish form of Urguist). If, as
is quite probable, his father had connections with a Dàl Riatan

ruling family, Oengus may have been engaged in a form of dynastic war on behalf of his own kindred, establishing them as subkings to himself. But the imposition on the Scots of Pictish laws is a new departure for 734 and does seem to mark Oengus's campaign as one to establish a Greater Pictland.

Following these events, Oengus was master of all the ancient Pictland, including the region that had become Dàl Riada. Unlike Kenneth MacAlpin, almost 100 years later, he did not set out to form a single kingdom. Although he is recorded as having enforced the laws of the Picts as against the laws of the Scots, which suggests that Pictish judges replaced or sat with the *brehons* of Scots tradition, he did not overturn the regional subkings. Despite his successful record as a war leader, Oengus was no mere warlord. What line he took with the Scots Church is not recorded, but Iona certainly was flourishing at this time, and some experts ascribe the making of the *Book of Kells*, in the scriptorium of Iona abbey, to his reign. The opulence of the work suggests high-level patronage, and the many Pictish references and influences in it have also been noted. The art of stone carving in Pictland was currently at a high point. It may have been in his reign and, if so, with his encouragement that the cult of St Andrew began, at a site anciently known as Mucros, 'moor or promontory of the pigs', on the eastern tip of Fife. Whatever the origin of the story of St Rule and his journey with the bones of the Apostle, it soon became clear that there was a cultic site on the east coast, rising, with royal support, to rival the renown of Iona and, while Iona was indubitably Scots in its origin as a Christian centre, this was equally plainly a Pictish foundation. The Picts did not cease to honour the memory of Columcille, but they also now had their own abbey under not only royal, but apostolic, patronage. The leaders of the Irish Church are not likely to have welcomed the new development. (It is possible that the dedication to St Andrew did not happen until much later, during the rule of Oengus II; the information available is by no means conclusive.)

Even before Oengus had completed his conquest of Dàl Riada, he was tested from the south. Around 740, Eadberct, king of Northumbria, led an invasion into Pictish territory, only to find his own country attacked from Mercia; following this, there was a Pictish-Mercian alliance. In 744, there was fighting between Picts and Strathclyde, perhaps with the Britons' northern frontier still in dispute. The men of Strathclyde defeated and killed Oengus's brother, Talorcan, in 750, in what was seen at the time as a significant battle; the Irish Annals recording 'the decline of the kingship of Oengus'. The historian, A. O. Anderson, suggested that, as a result of this battle, Teudubr, son of Bili, king of the Britons, became overlord of the Picts, a claim which the events of 756 do not seem to warrant. Teudubr died in 752 and, in the same year, there was an internal battle in the province of Circinn (Angus), in which the 'Annals of Tigernach' record the death of one Bruide son of Maelchu. He is believed to have been a leader of northern Picts: the victory in this civil war would appear to have been with Oengus. In 756, in alliance with Eadberct, Oengus invaded Strathclyde and reached as far as the Britons' chief stronghold at Dumbarton. But, even as the Britons appeared to be discussing surrender terms, they rallied, a battle ensued and Oengus was crushingly defeated. This appears to have been the last of his external adventures. He died in 761, and the Anglo-Saxon chronicle annexed to Bede's *History* commented on his life that he was 'a tyrannical murderer who from the beginning to the end of his reign persisted in the performance of bloody crime'. It is a surprisingly severe judgment on a king who does not appear to have been untypical of his age. But, unlike Nechtan, Oengus had been no friend of Northumbria and its churchmen. The cult of St Andrew was no more welcome to the Anglian Church, whose preferred saint was St Peter (the church built by the Anglian masons, probably at Restenneth in Angus, was dedicated to St Peter), than it was to the Irish Church. Oengus's last campaigns were, however, disastrous for

Pictland and undermined much of what he had achieved by his conquest of Dàl Riada.

Judges

Under Oengus's sway, the lands of Dàl Riada were ruled by tributary kings. By 748, Aedh Find, 'fair', son of Eochaidh, is noted by the annalists as king of the Scots. Oengus was succeeded by his brother Bredei, who died in 763, when Ciniod, recorded as the son of Uuredech, became king of the Picts. In 768, a battle was fought in the province of Fortriu between the armies of Aedh Find and Ciniod. The victor is not noted, but the event marks at least the existence of Aedh Find's campaign to restore the independence of Two years later, Ainbhceallach. He is recorded as a lawmaker. In the reign of Kenneth MacAlpin's successor, in the mid-ninth century, it is noted (M. Anderson, 189) that 'the Gaels with their king made the rights and the laws . . . of Aed son of Eochaid'; the Scots, having thrown out Oengus's laws when Aedh was their king, now, 100 years later, were imposing their own laws on the Scots-Pictish kingdom.

From the references made to king Oengus's imposition of Pictish laws on the conquered Scots of Dàl Riada in the mid-eighth century, it is clear that the Picts had a law system and that it was not identical to that of the Scots. What the laws were and how they were administered is not known. From the way in which contemporary references are framed, as 'laws of the Picts', it can be reasonably supposed that there was a general law code accepted throughout Pictish-inhabited territory. This, in turn, would require a cadre of professional lawmen – comparable to those known in the Irish tradition as *brehons*, 'judges' – to maintain and interpret it, and to give judgment. In this respect, there is no reason to suppose that the customs of the Picts were notably different to those of the Scots. Pictish place names, as has been noted, often display a concern with land areas, boundaries, and natural features. Land division, especially in countryside like that of Easter Ross, where the fertile coastal strip may be only one or two miles wide in places, was a vital matter. In addition, the taxation system was based on animals and produce, enhancing the value of good land. Laws defining and protecting tenure were necessary. Business transactions of other kinds and personal misdemeanours also had to be regulated or dealt with.

The Irish Gaels' law system, at least in its later stages, is much more fully recorded. Once imported to Scotland, it may have followed a separate line of development. Certainly, the Scots were capable of innovation, the most famous example being the 'Law of Innocents', proposed by abbot Adamnan of Iona in the late seventh century and brought to fulfilment by him at the Synod of Birr in Ireland in 697. This law was intended to exclude women and children from all warfare. Although its main aim was clearly to protect innocent victims, it is likely that it also forbade a practice that had been going on for centuries, that of women warriors. The tradition of this goes a long way back; reference has already been made to how in the 'Ulster Cycle' legends Cuchulainn and other heroes were trained in warfare by Scathach at her school for young warriors in Skye. The law was ratified by 40 senior clerics and 51 rulers, including king Bridei macDerilei of the Picts and Eochaid, king of Scots, as well as many subkings and chiefs. A note in the 'Annals' confirms its renewal in 727, when the saint's bones were transferred to Ireland. In fact, it partook of the nature of an international convention, rather than a traditional type of law. Its specific clauses and sanctions are not known. In a society that still retained and celebrated various forms of violence, it was a notable step forward, reflecting both the pastoral work of the Church and the ability of the leaders to accept change. They may, of course, as reformers often are, have been well ahead of popular opinion, if such a thing can be said to exist in seventh-century Scotland. The notion of the battling woman, like Black Agnes of Dunbar in the 14th century and Lilliard in the 16th, would continue to be much appreciated by the Scots.

The laws of the Irish were administered by officials of the druidical or priestly class; they were independent of the king. In Scotland, mention of the 'laws of Aedh Find' suggests more involvement on the king's part in the eighth century, unless his name is brought in merely to denote the era at which they were drawn up, or to emphasise that these were independent laws of the Scots. However, the way society was organised implies a definite role for the lawmen. From the individual family onwards, the structure of society was tribal, governed by kinship. A group of *tuatha*, or local tribes, combined to form a subkingship; all the subkings owed allegiance to a higher king. Thus the *cinele* of the Scottish kingdom were arranged. The king of Scots, as we have seen, was the king also of a *cineal*, usually that of Gabhràn, but sometimes that of Loairn. While a king might act impartially amongst his own people, he would not be expected to be impartial in a dispute involving another *tuath* or *cineal*. A trained man of law, omniscient on all questions of precedent and procedure, his person inviolate by sacred tradition, was needed to exercise impartial justice. The law was not the all-embracing thing it is today. Other regulatory systems operated within the society. In druidic times, the worst penalty for a wrongdoer was to be excluded from the rites; effectively, this turned the person out of the *tuath* and its protection. In the Christian period, excommunication by the Church had the same effect – another feature of life that would continue to produce vagrants and 'broken men' even in post-Reformation Scotland. The blood feud between families was a recognised event. In return for a death, or a deadly insult, honour and prestige required satisfaction. The key element was the family, or wider kindred. If a law was broken, it was not the individual malefactor who paid the fine; it was his family, or his *tuath*, paying shares determined by their rank; and the fine was correspondingly distributed among the offended family or *tuath*. Fines were normally payable in the form of cows. In this way, the kin group assumed both control of and responsibility for the actions of its individual members.

An alternative to the blood feud was the payment of an 'honour price', a practice known from the Irish and Britons, and likely to have been shared by Scots and Picts. The law provided a scale of charges to be paid, depending on the status of the person killed. Dr Nora Chadwick, in *The Celts*, draws attention to the institution of *galnes* (known in later Welsh as *galanas*), 'satisfaction for slaughter', among the Britons of Strathclyde, fixing payments to be made by the kin group. She also notes a post-eleventh-century compilation, *Leges Inter Brettos et Scottos*, 'Laws Between the Britons and Scots', based on laws pertaining to the Cumbrian province. By that time, of course, Strathclyde was being drawn into the polity of greater Scotland, and glosses on law and custom would have been essential for those who were in charge of bringing the different systems together.

The Crucible of Scotland

The lawgiving Aedh Find died around 778 and was followed by his brother, Fergus, who ruled for three years. After Fergus, the line of kingship is hard to trace until the appearance of Kenneth MacAlpin about 60 years later. It has been suggested that there was no single king of the Scots during this period. Such disunity would certainly have provided an opportunity for a Pictish king to re-establish Oengus's dominion over the Scots. But the Picts too appear to have been in disarray. Ciniod died in 775. After his reign, there may have been a period in which the Picts had no overking whose control covered the whole extent of Pictish territory – still the entire northern mainland and the islands. The cockpit was Fortriu, the Pictish province that bordered on Dàl Riada and that already had been substantially settled by Scots. To the south, it abutted on Strathclyde and Lothian. This area of mixed population could well claim to be the crucible in which Scotland's future was moulded. Fortriu was still a Pictish subkingdom, and one of the Pictish kings of the time, Talorcan or Dubtolargg, 'dark

Talorcan', is noted in the 'Annals of Ulster' as 'king of the Picts to the south of the Mounth' (M. Anderson, 191), implying that his authority did not extend to the north. There was strife among these petty kingdoms, within both the Scottish and the Pictish spheres and between them. One Conall, recorded around 805 as a king in Dàl Riada, appears to have been a Pictish king previously, until he was defeated in a battle with another Pictish king, Constantine, in 789. This Constantine, son of Uurguist (Fergus), ruled in Fortriu for a long time, until 820; Fergus is taken to be the king of Dàl Riada who died in 781. Conall's Gaelic name suggests that he also was of partly Scots descent. He was killed in Kintyre, around 807, by another Conall, who ruled in Dàl Riada until 811.

The intermarrying of ruling families of Scots and Picts, combined with the different laws of inheritance in each community, and the existence within each of centripetal tribal loyalties, had combined to create a situation where part-Pictish and part-Scottish rulers and would-be rulers could exercise conflicting claims on either side of the border. In such a situation, the traditional means of ensuring succession through the *derbfine*, tricky enough at any time, must often have been almost unmanageable. A mixed Scottish and Pictish population in Fortriu and Atholl further complicated matters. Since a claim to the kingship could not be backed up without an army, there must have been considerable movement of men from one side to the other. What was happening meanwhile in the great area of Pictland north and northwest of the Mounth is simply not known. If it was a separate Pictish kingdom or kingdoms at this time, it did not produce any ruler strong enough to impose himself on the disputants of the south. Eventually, from 789, Constantine emerges as the strong man. It appears likely that he combined the kingship of Fortriu with that of Dàl Riada between 811 and his death in 820. He was followed by his brother, Oengus II, who also ruled in both places, from the Fortrenn royal centre of Forteviot, until his death in 833.

Vikings

The 20 years of these two macFergus kings provided a degree of much-needed stability in the Fortriu-Dàl Riada kingdom. It was during this time that a profoundly unsettling new element entered into the world of Pict, Scot, Briton, and Anglian. Perceived at first as perhaps nothing more than a harassment, the raids of the Norsemen on the west coast began around 792. Between 795 and 806, Iona was attacked at least three times. By the latter date it was clear that the Norsemen were a very serious threat to all the established kingdoms of the British Isles. They were rapidly ceasing to be sporadic external raiders and forming a new, strong, and enduring element in the regional power structure. Their paganism added a sinister aspect to what, even by the standards of the time, was appalling brutality. With little space in their ships to take slaves, they killed males indiscriminately but carried off girls and women. Their language and their customs were equally strange (though less so to the Angles and Saxons). There is ample evidence that they were found to be utterly terrifying. The monasteries and religious hermitages of the Western Isles had been generally inviolate since around 617, when St Donnan, abbot of Eigg, and his community were killed by pagan Picts (interestingly, according to legend, ruled by a queen). They had no protection and the surprise nature of the raids made organised defence very difficult. No one could tell where the longships would strike next.

The macFergus rule has been seen as a re-establishment of Pictish dominion over the Scots, but the mixed ancestry of the kings, and the fact that they do not seem to have been kings of the whole of Pictland, do not justify this view. By the early ninth century, the Norsemen were settling in Orkney and Shetland, causing the existing population to take emergency measures, like the burying of treasures in the church on St Ninian's Isle (to be discovered in 1958). There is no record of any Pictish expedition to drive out the invaders. Such lethargy is not what might have been expected from a strong and united kingdom with a long tradition of rule or overlordship in the northern isles. The Picts had a well-established tradition as seafarers, though their curragh-type vessels were inferior to the clinker-built wood-plank longships. The lack of response suggests that there was no well-established central authority in the north at this time. Some evidence has been found of local resistance on the islands, with hastily thrown-up earthworks on promontory sites. But, by 820, hundreds of little farming-fishing settlements, with Norse names, were established in the islands. Their new proprietors might have gone off on 'summer raids' but they were essentially farmers with boats. Many of the Pictish islanders removed to the northern mainland – scholars are divided as to how much inte-gration there was between the incomers and the natives in the northern isles, but there can be no doubt that many Pictish com-munities were displaced. The record of Viking behaviour else-where suggests that, for those who could not leave, the future held the bleak alternatives of slavery or death.

Oengus II was succeeded in his Pictish domain by his nephew, Drest, son of Constantine, who seems to have shared power with one Talorcan, until 837. Whether, between the two of them, they controlled all of Pictland is not clear. From 837, the Pictish king list notes Uuen or Eoganan, son of Unuist or Hungus. In Dàl Riada, Oengus II was followed by Aed, son of Boanta, for some four years. But, from 837, Eoganan appears to have resumed the rule over both kingdoms that had been exercised by Oengus and Constantine.

Two years later, in 839, Eoganan was killed in a great inland battle against the Norsemen, along with a multitude of others, both Pict and Scot. In Dàl Riada, the kingship was perhaps briefly assumed by Alpin, said to be a grandson of Aedh Find, though his name is not recorded in the Irish Annals of the time. His son, Kenneth, possibly succeeded him but, in any case, successfully claimed the kingship of the Scots, in the same year.

CHAPTER FIVE

The Kingdom of Alba

Kenneth MacAlpin

Twice in the history of the Scottish kingdom, a strong and resolute man has seized the vacant throne, secured the allegiance of the people, and sufficiently legitimised his dynasty for his family to inherit the crown after him. The more famous one is Robert Bruce, who proclaimed himself king in 1306. His regime treated the preceding Balliol episode as an aberration, and official policy placed him firmly after Alexander III in the long line of kings of Scots that went back 500 years to Kenneth MacAlpin and beyond.

Kenneth was the other self-made king of Scots. For all its gaps and puzzles, the Bruce story is well recorded compared to his. From his name we know he was a Scot, the son of Alpin. In one of the source documents of early Scottish history, the eleventh-century 'Irish Synchronisms', this Alpin is named as a king of Scots, who reigned briefly between 832 and 834, and who was a member of the tribe of Fergus, of the race of Gabhràn. His ancestry could thus be traced back to Fergus macErc, the Dàl Riatan prince who led the Scottish colonisation of Argyll from Ulster around the year 500. It is an impeccable pedigree. Unfortunately, Alpin is a hazier figure than this record suggests. The other major sources, such as the 'Annals of Ulster', do not mention him at all, and it is likely that the record of his kingship is an official fiction, concocted to cover up Kenneth's lack of royal ancestry. The history of both Dàl Riada and Pictland is impossible to establish in clear detail in the period of 50 years or so before Kenneth's appearance. Around the year 839, the political situation was neither a clear-cut nor a comfortable one. The Norsemen, as raiders and land-seekers, were a serious threat to the three Celtic king-doms: Pictland, Dàl Riada, and Strathclyde. In response to this, Picts and Dàl Riadan Scots cooperated to resist the raids and invasions. But, at the same time, the Scots were pushing eastwards, into Pictish lands, partly, perhaps, to escape Viking raids and partly, perhaps, because their population was grow-ing too fast for their small territory. The political relations between the two are uncertain. It seems likely that, at this time, Dàl Riada, fast being eaten into by Viking colonists, was in effect a joint kingdom with that of the southern Picts. Each tribal or district group had its own local Scottish or Pictish chief or subking. Both main 'kingdoms' were some-what in flux, and whoever was king had only limited control over the numerous tribal groups that formed his people. But the defeat of 839 was a definitive event. When the joint Pictish-Scottish army was shattered in battle by a Viking force, not only Eoganan, king of the Picts and Scots, was killed, but also his brother, Bran. Another leader who died in the same fight was Aed, a Gaelic chief from Dàl Riada. It is probable that a number of other Dàl Riadan chiefs were present, either as free allies or as leaders of a summoned and dependent host, and that their number included Kenneth, son of Alpin. The uncertainty and disorder following such a drastic defeat could have provided a strong man with the opportunity to assert himself. The death of a king who had ruled both Scots and Picts, and perhaps the simultaneous deaths of potential suc-cessors, provided a chance for a subchief of the Dàl Riata to grasp at the leadership of that whole people.

No personal details of Kenneth have survived, other than the manner of his death, and his personality has to be reconstructed, as far as is reasonable, from his known actions. These make it clear that he was a man of exceptional ambition, energy, and ruthlessness. Without these qualities he would not have succeeded in becoming king of the Scots, a position he holds from 839. Even if there were no prime hereditary candidate for the position, there is never a lack of aspirants to an empty throne (Bruce's grandfather was to be one of 13 competitors in 1291). Even if he were not the son of a king, he must have come from the aristocracy of his people, able to claim royal blood from at least a great-grandparent; the intensely status- and honour-conscious Gaels would be most unlikely to accept a complete upstart as king. A further quality of Kenneth's might be suggested, and that is capacity for leadership, linked with proven military prowess. A champion was a greatly appreciated figure in the ninth century, even in normal times, and these were far from being normal times. The Picts and Scots had been experiencing increasingly heavy raids from seaborne Norsemen for more than a generation. In 818, Diarmaid, abbot of Iona, had felt it necessary to quit the vulnerable island, taking his community and its holy relics with him. And now the Norsemen were no longer merely raiding the coasts and islands, but conquering in a land campaign. Kenneth may have won renown in fighting off Viking raids on the Argyll coast, giving him the prestige as a war leader which his lineage perhaps could not provide, and also the support of the Scots warrior class. For the seniors of the Scots, the men who would expect to form a king's inner council, he may have appeared as the man most likely to maintain their position against both Picts and Vikings, as well as against the kingdom of Strathclyde and the powerful Northumbrians beyond. For a bold and ambitious man, it was a crucial moment. Kenneth seized it.

Already possessed of a commanding position among the Scots, he claimed the kingship of the Picts as well. Apart from the established tradition of joint kingship, two things may have helped him in this. One was that the Picts themselves were unable to produce an immediate and satisfactory successor to their own king. The other was perhaps that Kenneth himself could produce some evidence to legitimise what seems otherwise to be a breathtaking claim. It has been suggested that his mother was Pictish, though there is no proof to support this. A Highland historian wrote that:

'His own Pictish name and that of his son Constantine may indicate that he had such Pictish blood in his veins as gave him some claim to the throne.' (Mitchell, 136)

Certainly the name Kenneth, in its Gaelic form, Coinnich, does not occur in the lists of previous kings of Scots, whereas its Pictish forms, Cinaeth and Ciniod, both appear as predecessors in the Pictish king lists.

Whatever the validity of his claim, the new king did not find easy acceptance as ruler of both nations. The two peoples shared many similarities; their social systems were arranged on similar lines, in tribal family-based groups with clearly defined status and functions below the upper crust of an aristocratic warrior caste. But we do not know how vast the differences may have seemed. One was that of language. The relative closeness of Pictish and Gaelic was not enough to make them mutually intelligible. Such evidence as we have also points to some significant cultural differences between the peoples. From historical evidence in the king lists, it is clear that at least three Pictish challengers eventually appeared and had to be disposed of in battle. These were Kinat (Kenneth), son of Ferat or Feradach; Brude, son of Fotel; and Drost, also a son of Ferat. Their claim was based, perhaps more provably than Kenneth MacAlpin's, on family and, like his predecessors, they appear to have sought the kingship of both Picts and Scots. An intriguing possibility is that Drost is the person named in the inscription of the so-called 'Drosten Stone', still preserved at St Vigeans: *drosten, ipeuoret, ettforcus*. This has been tentatively translated as: 'Drost, son of Voret, of the race of Fergus', though only the three names are certain. It would proclaim an ancestry equal and akin to Kenneth's own pedigree, and also illustrate the degree to which ruling families of the Celtic nations were by then interrelated. Then, as later, they formed a virtually separate supercaste. The Pictish aristocracy clearly formed an actual or potential opposition to Kenneth. There is the persisting legend that he called the Pictish leaders to a feast and, having entertained them, had them all slaughtered when they were relaxed and merry with food and drink. The tale of such a feast at Scone is found in *The Prophecy of Berchàn*, whose origins are twelfth-century. Gerald of Wales in *De Instructione Principum* or 'The Teaching of Princes' (1214), gives a slightly more circumstantial account. It describes how the benches were specially constructed so that their underpinning could be removed and the helpless guests tipped backwards. But he quotes no authority, nor indeed any names. Some happening of the sort described is not improbable. But, though these stories about Kenneth may come from an earlier source, there is no surviving contemporary record of such an event. On the other hand, such a happening is a typical anecdotal story and, as such, is told of other usurping kings. Its purpose could be to make an otherwise almost inexplicable feat more comprehensible to the listening audience, or it might be a much-compressed conflation of the range of tactics that a king in Kenneth's situation would employ. Among such tactics were the propitiatory feasting of, and giving of rich gifts to, potential supporters among the chiefs and leading warriors. The assassination of proclaimed or anticipated rivals and their chief supporters would also be part of the process. If a rival had enough support to muster an army, then battle was inevitable.

Kinat, Brude, and Drost, two of them members of the same family, could certainly rely on support from their relatives and the forces their families controlled. The twelfth-century

Chronicle of Huntingdon, assembled from various earlier sources, records how, in 846, Kenneth 'encountered the Picts seven times in one day, and having destroyed many, confirmed the kingdom to himself.' This is seven years after his bid for the kingship. It was around this time that Drost, last of the rival claimants, was finally killed, either at Scone or Forteviot. Both these places were important centres of the Pictish kingdom, and his death may have been by execution rather than in battle.

Like his immediate predecessors, Kenneth made his power base not in Dàl Riada but at Forteviot, in lower Strathearn, nowadays a tiny crossroads hamlet whose 'holy hill', protected on the west by the Water of May flowing down to join the Earn, hardly suggests the location of a royal palace. But it was the royal centre of Fortriu, which, despite its mixed population of Scots and Picts, was certainly a Pictish province or subkingdom. At this time, of course, the old strongholds of the Dàl Riadan Scots – Dunadd, Dunollie, Dunstaffnage, and Tarbert – if in Scottish hands at all, were in a precarious situation. Most, if not all, of Dàl Riada would soon form part of the Norse kingdom of the Hebrides. But Kenneth was acting strategically, not simply acknowledging a tactical necessity. In this way he showed that his position was very different to that of any previous king who had ruled both peoples. The most recent example was the recently-dead Eoganan, who, though half-Scot, had emerged like his two predecessors from a Pictish context.

The previous ruler to these kings was the Pictish Oengus, who had conquered the Scots in 736. Although Oengus had imposed tributary status on the Scots and made them follow his laws rather than their own, he had ruled them at a remove, through Scottish subkings who had pledged their allegiance to him and insured it through providing him with hostages. While Kenneth could not dispense with the subkings or chieftains who were essential to the tribally organised society that he headed, it became clear that he was behaving as the ruler of a combined kingdom, not of two separate kingdoms. A comparison can be made with James VI of

Scotland on his accession to the throne of England in 1603. In theory, he could have ruled both countries from Edinburgh; in practical terms he knew that London was the real seat of power. In the same way, Kenneth was acknowledging the greater wealth, power, and security of Pictland, compared to Dàl Riada. Unlike James, whose attempts to make a full political union of his two realms were constantly frustrated, Kenneth was able to press on towards achieving this, though it was not completed in his life-time. He was also following an example set by a great many of his fellow-Scots, which was to move from the narrow glens and thin soils of the west into the wider, more fertile, and safer spaces to the east of the Drumalban ridge – there was now no bar to the Scots spreading through the vast and still relatively lightly, popu-lated region stretching from Strathearn to Fife and Angus.

Without Kenneth MacAlpin, would subsequent history have been different, or would the trend of events have brought about a single unified kingdom, even if Kenneth had died in 839 and his dynasty played no part in later events? The actions of individuals can certainly influence the course of national and international history. In Europe during the ninth century, there was already an uneven but distinct process towards the formation of national states out of former tribal domains, but this trend of events was anticipated rather than imitated by Kenneth's policy. At the time he was struggling to combine the Scottish and Pictish kingships, the European empire briefly formed under Charlemagne had fallen apart. France did not exist. England was soon to be partitioned by the Danelaw into Anglo-Saxon and Danish areas of control. Wales and Ireland, the countries most similar to Scotland, remained divided into tribal kingdoms, harassed (as was almost everywhere else in northern Europe) by Vikings. In both these latter countries, there would be a brief period when national unity seemed to be achieved, or almost achieved, in Ireland under Brian Bóruma, at the start of the eleventh century, and in Wales under Llywelyn ap Gruffudd in the thirteenth. But it did not outlast their lifetimes, while in Scotland, despite occasional falterings, political unity, as well as national cohesiveness, survived. Whether it would have failed in Scotland without Kenneth the reader may judge. But what stands out very clearly is the ferocious determination of MacAlpin, and most of his successors, to make that unity work and to build upon it.

The 'Disappearance' of the Picts

One aspect of the unification process has puzzled many people since Gerald of Wales became the first recorded writer to point it out: that of the two peoples it was the 'more warlike and significant one that disappeared'. The relative numbers of Picts and Scots are not known, but it has always been assumed that, with a far greater land area, the Picts were more numerous. But the difference, especially in the critical southern provinces, may not have been very great. A hybrid Picto-Scottish population may have grown up in Atholl and Fortriu. In any case, the Scots were not 'Picticised' and their identity, language, and culture prevailed. The way in which this happened is traced in the following pages. Certain factors were present from the start, however. One was the relative dynamism of the Scots: as has been noted, their ethos was that of colonists who had to impose themselves. They had brought Christianity, by now solidly established as the religion of the whole country. They had just become free of Pictish rule. In addition, a new and vigorous catalyst in the old compound of Pict, Scot, Anglian, and Briton had been provided by the Vikings. To the coastal and island kingdom of Dàl Riada they were a dire threat. The Scots had to move, had to transfer their seat of power to somewhere more secure. Pictland's southern provinces, already with a strong Scottish element in their population, were the obvious location. The Scots had to establish themselves there, or be squeezed to extinction between Norsemen and Picts. The personal qualities of Kenneth MacAlpin, and his successors,

ensured their survival. After that, the only way was forward, to
further hegemony. Not just the kingdom, but also the nation of
Scots would cease to exist unless, like a small huge-mouthed
fish successfully engulfing a prey larger than itself, it took over
the institutions of the kingdom of Picts.

No doubt, at the time it often appeared as a fraught and vulnerable enterprise, a huge gamble centred on the life, ability, and
determination of one man. It took many years and many tears
before the Picts and Scots came to consider themselves a single
nation. Three hundred years on from Scotland's union with
England of 1707, the sense of two nations remains. Three hundred years after Kenneth MacAlpin, the old Pictish provinces
were giving plenty of trouble to the centralised Scottish crown.
But then, so were regions with a long Gaelic tradition, like the
Western Isles. Local warlords always preferred independence to
interference, and would brandish the Pictish or British tradition
to help them maintain it. But there was no movement for a
Pictavia Irredenta. By 1034, Picts and Scots were combined in a
Gaelic-speaking nation. In the north of Ireland, the Picts, no
longer a political reality, suffered the same fate as some earlier
vanished peoples: they became creatures of folk myth, the
ground-dwelling, half-magic *pechts*.

The MacAlpin Consolidation

Kenneth MacAlpin had made himself king of two peoples who
were already accustomed, at least in the south, to being ruled
jointly by a king with family connections on each side. There
were also compelling strategic reasons for solidarity and
alliance in the face of the Viking invasions. Nevertheless, it is
clear that Kenneth was not accepted as a legitimate king of the
Picts: he had to impose himself, and the process was not a
peaceful one and took several years, at least until 847. How far
into the remoter Highlands Kenneth's authority ran we do not
know. It was important for him to establish control over as

much territory as possible, since already the far north of the mainland and the Hebrideswere being colonised by Norsemen. It was also vital to establish the policy of the new Scots-Pictish kingdom towards Strathclyde, Northumbria, the Norse colonies, and the powerful but remoter Anglo-Saxon kingdoms such as Mercia and Wessex.

Kenneth also needed to consolidate his regime at the centre. Iona, though it was to be sporadically reoccupied by Irish monks, could no longer function as the effective headquarters of the Church. In 825, there was a horrific raid when St Blathmac, who had returned with some followers to the holy island, was bloodily murdered by treasure-seeking Vikings; it shows the abbot's earlier departure to have been prudent. The functions of the monastery were transferred to Kells in Ireland, although this was seen as a temporary measure. Some of the relics and, it may be supposed, the monastic scribes' work-in-progress, were brought to Kells, others to the Scottish mainland. It was necessary to accommodate these, and to create a new religious centre in a less exposed place. The 'family' of Iona, expelled from Pictland by Nechtan in 717, returned after more than a century, to re-establish their way of doing things. Constantine had already established a church in Dunkeld. Kenneth appears to have refounded this establishment and endowed it with more of Columba's relics. In a tenth-century battle against the Vikings, the *cathal*, 'crook' of Columba, known as the *Cath Bhuaidh*, 'battle victory', was carried before the army. The still-extant *Brecbennoch*, the little reliquary said to have contained fragments of bread blessed by the saint (Mitchell, 215), had already been made by this time. There were a number of significant churches in Pictland, at Kilrymont (the later St Andrews), Abernethy, Brechin, Banchory, and Restenneth among others; there were also the northern monasteries at Rosemarkie, Fearn and Applecross, in areas eventually to be subject to Norse earls. These foundations, Applecross apart, were of the Pictish Church. Kenneth clearly found it necessary, or preferable, in 850

to establish his 'own' central church and to equip it with prestigious relics rather than to borrow the prestige of an existing
church. The next two centuries would see some further competition employing saintly names, Andrew, Columba, and Ninian,
as the structure of Church government evolved. To Kenneth, the
important thing politically was the Church's role as a part of his
government system, as an integral part of national life, and also as
the guarantor of his own legitimacy as ruler. This latter consideration was not likely to be on offer from senior clerics of the
Pictish Church. The circumstances of his formal installation as
king of the Picts are not recorded.

Marital links with neighbouring states were established. One
of Kenneth's three daughters married Rhun, who was to become
king of the Strathclyde Britons, another may have married Aedh
Finnliath, high king of Ireland, and the third was wedded to a
Norwegian, Olaf the White, joint king of Dublin. (Some time
before or, perhaps in the interest of this political match, Olaf had
repudiated his first wife, Aud, 'the Deep-Minded', daughter of
Ketill Flatnose.) Kenneth's southward policy was aggressive: he
attacked Lothian and Bernicia in 850, burning Dunbar and
Melrose. In the *Scalachronica* it was recorded that:

'He subjected to his government the whole country to the
Tweed, expelled the Angles and Britons who inhabited it,
and caused the country to be called Scotland . . . '

Despite the dynastic marriage, there was no peace with the
Britons. They are recorded as invading and burning Dunblane.
Dunkeld itself was attacked by Danish raiders during Kenneth's
reign. A. P. Smyth has, however, explored some interesting
aspects of Kenneth's relations with the Hebridean Norsemen.
Already by this time the *Gall-Gaedhil*, literally, 'foreigner-Gaels',
a people compounded of Norse and Irish-Scots stock, were a
significant power in the Western Isles. Although independent,
they leant more towards support of Norse than Celtic kingdoms,

but Smyth suggests that their king Guthfrith, who died around 853, had been enlisted as an ally by Kenneth as early as 836.

Kenneth MacAlpin died around 858, at his power base of Forteviot. In an unusual venture into medical detail, the 'Pictish Chronicle' states that he died *tumore ani*, 'of a tumour of the rectum'. According to tradition, he was buried on Iona. He was succeeded by his brother, Donald, apparently without difficulty. A significant event of Donald's reign, and one that shows an extension of Scottish custom and practice into Pictland, was the proclamation at Forteviot that the laws of the Gaels – defined as those of Aedh Find, the Dàl Riadan king who had ended the Pictish suzerainty – should be the laws of the kingdom. Donald was followed in 863 by Kenneth's son Constantine I. This imperial-sounding name was clearly a well-considered one, to establish a link with the previous Constantine, another ruler of both peoples and a Pict into the bargain, as well as with the Roman emperor, whose personal links with Scotland would have been well remembered. Constantine was followed by his son Donald. The Scots had imported their system of succession to Pictland, but this son-follows-father sequence underlines the isolation of the House of Alpin, both from Scottish and Pictish alternative royal lines, or at least its determination to establish its own *derbfine* as the source of future kings. The family grip was determinedly tight. Even the Danish occupancy of vast areas of prime land during Constantine's kingship would not dislodge its hold on the crown. In 878, though, it became clear that the MacAlpin *derbfine* was no more united within itself than any previous one. Aed, second son of Kenneth MacAlpin, who became king on the death of his brother Constantine I, was defied by his first cousin, Giric, the son of Donald I. In a battle that same year, Aed was killed. Giric was supported by his Strathclyde second cousin Eochaid (son of king Rhun and Kenneth MacAlpin's daughter) who co-ruled with him until 889, when they were both deposed and Donald II, son of Constantine, assumed the kingship. Donald II was followed in

900 by his first cousin, Constantine II, the son of the assassinated Aed. Despite this fighting like cats in a bag among the
descendants of Kenneth, it is notable that no other family,
Pictish or Scottish, was able to enforce a claim on the kingship.

A prime concern for the king, at this time still described in
the Annals as *rex Pictorum*, 'king of the Picts', and his advisers
was to keep up to date with events among the Viking kingdoms, and decide how to cope with them. Through the last
three quarters of the ninth century it was the struggle and fluc-
tuating power balance between Viking states, chiefly those
based in Dublin and in York, which drove political and military
events throughout the British Isles. Whatever his father's relations with the Hebridean-based Vikings had been, in
Constantine I's time, the Gall-Gaedhil, under their chief, Ketill
Flatnose, emerged as open enemies. Pirates and raiders, their
aim was for plunder rather than conquest, but they were a
plague to exposed coastal communities both in Scotland and in
Ireland. They straddled the Norway-Dublin communications
route, which was vital to the Dublin Norse colony.

In 853, Olaf the White, son of the Norwegian king of
Vestfold, was sent to Dublin to clear the seas of the Gall-Gaedhil
and, by 857, he had largely succeeded. With a seasoned galley
fleet and fighting force, he was then free to consider other activities. In 866, despite his marriage to Kenneth's daughter, Olaf
himself led an invasion force into southern Pictland, while his
co-ruler Ivar invaded England; and he may have remained in
Fortriu for as long as three years. Olaf was a plunderer rather
than a kingdom-builder, fortunately for the Scots. The effects
on their kingdom, and what Constantine did in that time, are
unclear, but he either came to terms with the pagan 'squatters'
or, less probably, withdrew into the province of Circinn (Angus)
to preserve some sort of independence. The Scottish-Pictish
state survived, and the Vikings finally departed. In 871, Olaf was
again on the attack, this time with Ivar against the Britons at
Dumbarton. Their successful siege effectively marked the end

of the independent kingdom of Strathclyde, and events a few years later suggest that the Scots were in league with the Vikings. The invaders returned to Ireland with vast amounts of plunder and many slaves but, once again, do not seem to have tried to consolidate their victory. Olaf's attention after that appears to have been focused back in the Norwegian kingdom of Vestfold, and, as A. P. Smyth surmises, he may have been the king buried in the fine and splendidly preserved Gokstad Ship. After Olaf's withdrawal, the hostile pressures from Dublin ceased for a time but, for an uncomfortably long period, it must have seemed as though the combined Scoto-Pictish kingdom might be destroyed by Norse aggression from south and north.

The Norse Occupancy

In the far north of the mainland, Thorstein the Red, a grandson of Ketill, and a son of Olaf the White by Aud, his first wife, battled in the early 870s to set up a kingdom for himself. Whatever the extent of rule by the king at Forteviot or Scone over this region, the opposition to Thorstein appears to have been entirely on a local basis, mounted by Pictish chiefs or subkings and their people. Many refugee Picts from the northern isles may have also resettled in the northern mainland. Resistance to this further Norse onslaught was strong. Thorstein had hardly established his control of Caithness and Sutherland when he was defeated and killed by the Picts around the year 876, and his mother, Aud the Deep-Minded, eventually sailed for Faeroe and then Iceland, where a new Norse community was founded. It is unclear whether the Picts regained all of Thorstein's conquest, and to what extent Norse settlers remained, but it seems that Sigurd, second jarl of Orkney under the Norwegian king Harold Haarfagr, had to reconquer the same territory, though on behalf of his royal superior rather than as a personal domain. According to the sagas of later date, the Orkney Vikings, an anarchic collection of pirates and raiders, who had been attacking

their own erstwhile homeland as well as Scotland, were assailed
by Harold Haarfagr with the aid of Rognvald of Möre, whom
he made first jarl of Orkney. Modern historians have doubted
Harold's campaign, and suggested that the Möre family had
established itself independently around 860. But from 890 or
some years before, the northern isles were incorporated into
Harold's unified Norwegian kingdom. The jarldom was passed
to Rognvald's brother Sigurd, who met his death around 890
after a semilegendary battle with Maelbrigte, a Pictish subking
of Moray. Sigurd's force won the battle (through treachery,
according to legend), but Maelbrigte had a protruding tooth,
which, as his decapitated head swung from the jarl's saddle,
scratched Sigurd's leg and caused a wound which went septic
and killed him.

Caithness, the coastal areas of Sutherland, and Easter Ross
remained Norse territory, and only frantic fighting kept Sigurd
out of Moray. Sigurd's son Guthorm briefly held the jarldom
of Orkney before his death, when the position was given to
Rognvald's youngest son, Einar, about 895. Known as *Torf-
Einar*, 'Turf-Einar', from his encouragement of the use of peat
as fuel, Einar completed the task of clearing out nests of piratical Vikings from the islands. The Scottish kings seem to have
played no part in these northern events; indeed the historian
Hume Brown noted that the Norwegians' mainland earldom
was 'in truth in the interests of the kings of Scots themselves.
To the north of the Grampians they exercised little or no
authority; and the people of that district were as often their
enemies as their friends' (*History of Scotland*, i, 27). For the time
being, the distraction of the rulers of Moray by the activities of
the northern Vikings may have seemed a good thing, enabling
the kings of Scots to focus their main attention southwards.

To the south, the Danes were rapidly establishing control over
the former Anglian kingdom of Northumbria, which brought
them into direct conflict with the Norwegians of Dublin.
Conscious of where he was most vulnerable, Constantine allied

himself with the Dublin kingdom, but events overtook him. In 874–5, there was an invasion from the south by the Viking leader Hálfdan, brother of the Dublin king Ivar, who had died in 873. Hálfdan had taken control of York. In 875, he is recorded as having massacred the Picts, in a battle that may have taken place below the Ochil Hills at Dollar.

The battered kingdom of Strathclyde in those years was a highway for Norse armies coming and going between York and Dublin, using the short sea route from the western edge of Galloway. The struggle went on, and in 877, Constantine I was killed fighting the Danes, the second king in the ninth century to die in this way. The place is recorded as Inverdufatha, identified tentatively as present-day Inverdovat, in Fife. Like Olaf before him, Hálfdan did not withdraw but remained in Pictland for a year. Unlike Thorstein in the north, he was the master of a roving war–band, rather than of a community that desired to settle, and Danish colonists did not follow in his wake. Constantine was able to sit him out. Eventually he fell out with the captains of his own York-centred war band, and was killed trying to establish himself in control of Dublin in 877.

In Northumbria, the Angles still clung to the rock of Bamburgh and maintained a shaky control over the old kingdom of Bernicia. Events in this region were dictated not by the Scoto-Pictish kingdom but by the dynamic of power within the Norse colony, whose Dublin and York bases sometimes formed an axis and sometimes mutually hostile camps. More menacing in the longer term was the consolidation of the power of Wessex to the south. The son of Alfred the Great, Edward the Elder, sought to build on his father's work and that meant inevitable confrontation with the York Danes. In the time of Constantine II, the Scots would be drawn into this struggle. The Pictish 'buffer' remained in the north, where some kind of stability in relations with the Norwegian jarldom had set in and, if there was conflict, there was also trade, the interpenetration of language, and the exchange of royal brides.

The Decline and Fall of Strathclyde

The year after the Dublin Vikings' sacking of the fortress of
Dumbarton, the king of Strathclyde, Artgal, who had survived
the devastation. was killed 'on the advice of Constantine, son
of Kenneth macAlpin'. The circumstances of this murder or
execution in 872 are unexplained, but imply a degree of control by Constantine over Strathclyde's internal affairs. Artgal
was succeeded as king of Strathclyde by Rhun. After Eochaid,
son of Rhun, no further Britons are recorded as kings of
Strathclyde. The next is Owen, who, despite his Brittonic
name, is a son of Donald II, king of Scots, and from then until
1034 – when the kingship of Strathclyde comes to an end – the
kings are from the house of MacAlpin. Scarcely two generations away from the coup that established them as kings of
Picts as well as of Scots, this redoubtable family added the
third of the Celtic kingdoms of North Britain to its empire.

It was a remarkable achievement, rivalling that of the
Hautevilles in Apulia and Sicily, or that of any other Norman
dynast of the next century. The kingdom of Strathclyde, which at
times had been the predominant one in North Britain, had suffered greatly in the ninth century because of its position, lodged
between the two great Norse power bases. The development of
English-speaking states in South Britain had effectively cut it off
from its fellow-speakers of the 'Old Welsh' tongue which in
Wales was developing towards the modern Welsh language.
Contact with Wales by sea was made hazardous by the Vikings'
control of the western seaways. Cut off culturally and politically,
Strathclyde was vulnerable. The Gall-Gaedhil had established
themselves on its southwestern edge (the name Galloway, found
as Galweya in the tenth-century 'Pictish Chronicle', means 'land
of the stranger-Gaels'). In the north, Picts and Scots were moving into the Lennox, in the hinterland of the once-impregnable
Ail-Clutha, 'Rock of Clyde', on which the Britons' main fortress
stood. Places and features that had borne Cumbric names for

centuries were renamed by the new arrivals; other old names survived. Near to Gaelic-named Stranraer, 'wide promontory', is Dunragit, the Cumbric 'fort of Rheged', preserving the name of what had been at times a province or subkingdom of a vibrant Strathclyde. Even now, its boundaries still reached to the southern edge of the Lake District. On the coast south of Cumbric Dumfries, 'fort among the trees', the Solway Firth, 'fjord of the mud banks', bears the name given by the Norsemen, replacing its old Cumbric name of Echwydd, 'tide flow'. At the head of the Solway, numerous landward places also bear Danish names, witness to the fact that the Norsemen had not merely tramped through, but had settled.

In Strathclyde, the Scots did not seek the kind of integration that they had forced on Pictland. The kingdom of Strathclyde was maintained. While this may have been convenient in providing another kingship for the expanding families of Kenneth MacAlpin's descendants, that was unlikely to be the reason. Indeed the establishment of a separate family power base had obvious risks (the next century would see family wars between Alba and Strathclyde). The violent usurpation by Giric in 878 showed that the son of Donald MacAlpin had no confidence in being allowed his turn by the sons of Kenneth, his first cousins. Perhaps the administration of a third kingdom, with yet another language and yet another cultural background, seemed to make the task of government too complex. More probably, it was because the extreme pressures that had existed in 839, with the Vikings pushing hard into Dàl Riada, were no longer present. There was no reason for a fusion of the kingdoms; to install a Scottish king was the natural, as well as the easiest, option. The disaster of 871 is likely to have partially destroyed the aristocracy of Strathclyde, creating a vacuum of power which immigrating Scots could readily fill. The curiously described killing of the British king Artgal, on Constantine's advice, suggests that he was already in the power of the Scottish king. His successor, Rhun, bound by a marriage tie to the Scots, may have been a client-king. Eochaid's pact with Giric, however, suggests a degree of freedom of action. Recent archaeological work has revealed that Govan, a few miles up river, may have replaced Dumbarton as the royal centre. The existence of a road leading from the old churchyard to the artificial mound of 'Doomster Hill' nearby has been compared with the layout of the Tynwald in the Isle of Man, and suggests that a Norse influence was also present. The kingdom of Man was still under Norse control and would remain so until the twelfth century. A need to take account of this Norse political influence may also have played a part in maintaining Stathclyde's separate structure.

The alliance of Eochaid and Giric lasted for eleven years. During this period, Giric campaigned successfully in Bernicia against the Danes; indeed, exaggerated accounts in Scottish medieval chronicles would tell of his having conquered Ireland and the greater part of England (Mitchell, 149). In 889, both Giric and Eochaid were forcibly deposed in another family upheaval that brought Donald II, son of Constantine I, briefly to the throne before his death in 900. This event is attested in Version A of the 'Scottish Chronicle', and seems the best explanation of events, accepted as such by A. P. Smyth, though A. A. M. Duncan believes that Eochaid and Giric were rivals and Giric died naturally at the fortress of Dundurn. The lengthy reign of Constantine II, son of the assassinated Aed, followed in the Scottish-Pictish kingdom, while Donald II's son, Owen, became king of Strathclyde. A centripetal strain was very clear in the MacAlpin clan: the further away a family member was from the line of descent that ran from Kenneth through Constantine I, Donald II and Malcolm I, the less likely he was to become king.

Whether or not Eochaid had eligible relatives, the event of 889 was decisive. It was clearly seen by the Britons as a Scottish assumption of power, and many of them, particularly the chiefs and the warrior class, with their bards, historians, and priests, removed to join their kindred in Wales at that time, settling on the eastern border. The process of 'Scotticisation' intensified as the upper and learned classes of Scots moved in to occupy the duns and houses abandoned by their British counterparts, and to establish the laws and customs with which they themselves were familiar. This process was not swift and areas of Cumbric speech remained, probably into the twelfth century. The bestowal of Cumbric names like Rhyderch and Owen on some of the later rulers of Strathclyde may imply a continuing need to make Scottish control more tolerable by giving it a Cumbric tone. Alternatively, it could indicate a degree of reverse influence, a 'Cumbricisation' of the Scots, rather as the later Normans would eventually become Gaelicised in both Scotland and Ireland, adapting to both language and custom in their new domains. Later surnames in the region, such as Welsh and Wallace, testify to the continuing British strain in the population; they come from the Anglian word for 'foreigner'. For several centuries, Galloway in particular would be a province seen by itself and by outsiders as distinct in its identity and customs. This owes more to the legacy of the Gall-Gaedhil than to that of the Britons, but it testifies to the slow and patchy impact of Scottish rule. Professor Duncan notes that, as late as 1034, the annalists could record the death of a 'king' (*ri*) of the Gall-Gaedhil. Undoubtedly, one result of the Gall-Gaedhil settlement was to establish an essentially pagan Gaelic-speaking society in the far southwest, by the back door, as it were.

The Moray Faction

Constantine II was to be king for 43 years. His predecessor, Donald II, had fought against Viking raids or invasions at Dunottar, and is recorded as having died at Forres. This is the first indication of a king of Scots being active in northern Pictland. It must be assumed that Donald was asserting his rights there as overking. It has also been surmised that, by this time, the rulers in Moray were not of Pictish origin but were in fact Scots, descended from members of the Cineal Loairn, who had finally succeeded in pushing northeast through the Great Glen into the fertile lowlands of Moray, where they established themselves as a ruling element. In *Kings and Kingship in Early Scotland*, Marjorie Anderson notes:

> 'Certainly the "kings" of Moray in the eleventh century traced their descent from the Cenél Loairn, as the kings of Scots traced theirs from Fergus son of Erc.'

The establishment of a new Gaelic-Pictish power centre would not be something that a MacAlpin king could afford to tolerate (in *Lost Kingdoms*, J. L. Roberts places this establishment as early as the reign of Kenneth MacAlpin himself). The long hostility between the royal houses of Moray and the MacAlpins was not about Pictish separatism but over possession of the whole kingdom of Alba; the northerners would triumph for a time with the reign of Macbeth, before Malcolm III, with English help, would retrieve the throne for Kenneth's line. But the early years of Constantine II's reign were also plagued by Norse attacks on his own territory. These reached as far as Dunkeld in 903–4 and, while the Scots successfully resisted these raids, defeating a Norwegian army in Strathearn in 904, there is no evidence that Constantine paid much attention to the north. He did maintain the MacAlpin tradition of abolishing Pictish official practices in favour of those of the Scots. During the reign of Giric and Eochaid, it had been proclaimed that the Scottish Church had been liberated from the servitude of the law and custom of the Picts. W. F. Skene explains this as a legal and fiscal matter, concerned with the Church lands. Following the expulsion of the Columban clergy in 716, the Pictish churches had come increasingly under secular control, and the freedom of Church lands from tax-paying and other servitudes had been greatly infringed by the local chiefs. Now the freedom of Church lands from all dues was restored throughout the kingdom. A few years later, in 908, there was a solemn ceremony at Scone, in which king Constantine II and Cellach, the first recorded bishop of St Andrews, jointly vowed to 'protect the laws and discipline of the faith, and the rights of the churches and of the Gospel, equally with the Scots'.

The Cult of St Andrew

From the beginning of the seventh century, Iona had been the Christian centre of what still remained of the Celtic world – by this time confined to the British Isles and to the northwestern tip of Gaul. This role, as we have seen, was not supported by anything other than the Columban tradition and the natural authority and important connections of its abbots. Abbeys like Bangor or Clonmacnoise in Ireland would have considered themselves equal or superior at the time, with a longer history, just as great a teaching and missionary achievement, and probably a larger population of monks and laymen. Iona's pivotal location, with hindsight, makes it unique, and episodes like the adopting of the Law of Adamnan show the role it could play in bringing many different political groups together. As far as the Church in Dàl Riada was concerned, Iona's supremacy was unchallenged. The position in Strathclyde and Pictland is more complex. First in Whithorn, then in Glasgow, the Britons had created their own ecclesiastical centres and endowed them with the prestige of Ninian and Kentigern, and a history that ante-dated Iona's. When, after the Scottish takeover of 889, the aristocracy of Strathclyde evacuated itself to Wales, the leading priests and monks would have gone too. In the south, the influence of Durham, already established along the coast, was then able to penetrate further, forming the basis for a later claim of ecclesiastical supremacy over Scotland.

The Pictish Church, on the other hand, was very much a daughter of the Scottish one. In the 'Pictish Chronicle''s reference to the founding of Abernethy, the oldest record (if genuine) of a Church in Pictland, the eminent Irish abbess, Darlugdach of Kildare, was invited to bless the foundation and it was dedicated to Kildare's St Bridget. Until the appearance of the St Andrew story, some time after the founding of the monastery at St Andrews, the Picts had no metropolitan Church. Nor did they have a great teaching monastery like those of Iona and Ireland. Pictish monks would go through their novitiates in Gaelic monasteries (and some also in Strathclyde and Wales). Yet the structure of the Pictish Church was aligned with the structure of the Pictish realm and its sub-divisions; and its senior churchmen were very much part of the machinery of government. We do not know what propor-tion of the Pictish clergy were native Picts and whether these were among the 'family of Iona' expelled by king Nechtan in 717. Possibly the thought of senior clerics as strangers within the walls speeded up such developments as that of the lay abbot, who exercised abbatial authority, including control of its tenants, in secular matters.

In Volume 2 of *Celtic Scotland*, W. F. Skene spends some time considering the St Andrew legend and its origins. He looks at the different versions of the story, and equates St Regulus, the bringer of the relics, with the early seventh-century Irish saint, Riagail, whose island, Mucinis, 'pig isle', has a certain affinity in name with old Mucros, 'promontory of pigs', where St Regulus is said to have landed. This attribution is denied by Dr Isabel Henderson in *The Picts*. She also casts doubt on Skene's view that the Church dedicated to St Andrew was founded by a Northumbrian bishop, Acca, who was expelled from his own see of Hexham in 732. Nevertheless, Skene pro-duces some strong circumstantial evidence. Acca was known as an ardent collector of holy relics, including some relating to St Andrew, and he was recorded as having gone to the country of the Picts. In advancing this view, Skene was, no doubt, aware that the origin he suggests would be unpalatable to many Scots. Hexham had been founded by St Wilfred, the ambitious Anglian enemy of the Celtic Church and of the Picts, and Wilfred dedicated his church there to St Andrew because he believed St Andrew had helped him develop his powers of eloquence. Even Scots who regard the St Regulus story as a myth may not like to think they owe the cult of their patron saint not merely to St Wilfred but to that very oratorical quality of his that helped him defeat the Celtic Church at the Synod of Whitby. They would prefer the St Andrew story to be home-grown. Dr Henderson would not be influenced by such a consideration, but her refutation rests chiefly on the fact that 'there is no record of a dedication to St Andrew at Kilrymont before the tenth century'. It does not mean that there was no such dedication before the tenth century, but she is correct in accepting nothing without actual proof.

The early Celtic Church retained a reputation for the purity of its spirit. Nevertheless, there were some clerics who failed to maintain the standard. Bede records the destruction by fire of the convent of Coldingham, around 680:

' . . . it happened because of the wickedness of its members, and in particular of those who were supposed to be in authority.'

The burning was foreseen by an ascetic Celtic monk. By this time, the Church was long established and it would be no surprise to see signs of degeneracy entering into its systems and practices, and equally unsurprising to see evidence of corrective measures. During the ninth century, and originating in Ireland, a reform movement grew within the church, possibly in reaction to the kind of backsliding noted at Coldingham. There had, of course, been monastic communities ever since the church was formed but, in the late eighth century, St Maelruan, abbot of Tallaght, a monastery just outside the walls of Viking Dublin, drew up a rule of life for members of his community.

They were known as the *Ceile Dé*, 'companions of God', secular priests living according to a monastic rule but without having taken monastic vows. The *Ceile Dé*, their name Latinised as *Colidei* and, in English, as Culdees, had earlier been holy hermits; now they formed communities particularly in association with cathedral or collegiate churches. Until the introduction of the European monastic orders in the twelfth century, the Culdees would continue to serve the abbey and priory churches of Scotland. Though later, partly perhaps through hostile propaganda, they had a reputation for laxness, there is no reason to doubt their austerity and sanctity in the ninth and tenth centuries.

The people themselves undoubtedly preserved a host of pre-Christian attitudes, beliefs, and practices. Unconcerned with the whole complex schema of Christian theology, they fastened on certain key figures, particularly the Virgin Mary, St Michael, and Christ the King, as totemic sources of protection against the ills and fears of daily life. Although St Columba warned against such things, a deep fascination with charms and omens remains apparent in Gaelic folklore and literature:

> 'I pray and with my supplication sue
> To druid Coivi and Columba true,
> I pray unto the Mother of my King,
> To modest Bridget maid petitioning,
> To Michael of the warfare I make prayer,
> High king he is of soldiers of the air,
> That they give succour and they shield me round
> From all the little folk of fairy mound.'

This invocation, adapted from Alexander Carmichael's *Carmina Gadelica*, collected in the later 19th century, is typical in its mingling of Christian and pre-Christian elements. Books like Anne Ross's *The Folklore of the Scottish Highlands* are rich in examples of pagan and semipagan taboos, cures, incantations, and seasonal rites, which survived until the 17th or 18th centuries, and some of which still remain.

While the event at Scone in 908 has been seen as the final triumph of the Columban Church, nearly 200 years after its expulsion from Pictland, the facts are less facile. Dunkeld had been chosen by Kenneth MacAlpin as the place for some of Columba's relics to be laid, and its abbot had been appointed Bishop of Fortriu, head of the Pictish Church. Its cathedral might have been seen as the new Columban mother church. However, it seems that on the death of Tuathal, the first bishop of Fortriu, in 865, king Constantine transferred the bishopric from Dunkeld to Abernethy. In the *Scotichronicon*, Walter Bower states that three bishops were elected from there and that it was 'at that time the principal royal and episcopal seat, for some time, of the whole kingdom of the Picts' (Skene, ii, 310). Abernethy had, for centuries, been an important Pictish centre. But, from 906 at least, under its first known bishop, Cellach, it was St Andrews which became the ecclesiastical capital. It was under a Pictish king that the rise of St Andrews had begun, and the whole St Andrew legend is very much a Pictish property. Cellach is a Gaelic name but it is likely that, by now, though Pictish names also continued to be in use, many of the leading class would give their sons Gaelic names and Cellach may have been a Pictish, rather than a Columban, priest, though the latter is more likely. It was thus a Pictish foundation that became the metropolitan centre of the Scottish Church, and the legend of the patron saint of the Picts triumphed over the history of such indigenous saints as the Briton Ninian and the Gael Columba who brought the gospel. In this respect, Scotland was unlike Wales and Ireland, whose prime evangelists also became their patron saints. Constantine II's favour for St Andrews was clear. Having relinquished the kingship, it is here, to the monastery of Kilrymont, that he would make a distinguished retirement in 943.

The Church and the institutions of state, religion, and policy, remained closely intertwined. The ascendancy of St Andrews, at

the eastern extreme from Iona (then still in the Norse-
Hebridean kingdom) and Ireland, is significant in terms of policy. Despite their proudly claimed origins in the Cineal
Gabhrain, the kings of Scots at this time had little to do with
their distant Gaelic relations in Ireland. Their allies were the
usurping Dublin Vikings. The Gaelic kingdoms of Ireland,
despite the institution of the High Kingship, at this time
remained a disparate set of provincial groups, often at mutual
war, often acting in alliance with the Vikings who possessed
Dublin, Limerick, and Waterford. Intent on the consolidation of
their power, the kings of Scots saw little value in alliance with
the petty kingdoms of tenth-century Ireland. The ancient
Columban connection with the Úi Néill had lost its prestige.
The cult of St Andrew proclaimed and sustained a new political,
and ultimately national, identity.

The Withering of Pictish

These were the actions of a governing group that clearly knew
what it was doing, even if its reasoning can only be guessed at.
In pressing on with the Sscotticisation of law and Church practice, it was not being narrowly tradition-minded. It seems
improbable that the St Andrew cult was, in any intended way, a
sop to Pictish feelings; rather, it was seen as the right way forward for a ruling elite that was focused on the realities of power
and position. Much thought and speculation has been devoted
to the loss of the Pictish language and of Pictish cultural characteristics during this period. Many people have been surprised
that the language of the Scots, spoken by (it is presumed) fewer
people, should have replaced that of the Picts. It is most
unlikely that the MacAlpin regime ever tried to stamp out the
use of Pictish. Such a policy would have been extremely difficult to put into effect. But it was also unnecessary. Law (including the laws of inheritance, ownership, and boundary
defining), religion, administration, and military organisation,

were all taken from Scots practice and framed in the Gaelic language. However devoted to their own language they might be, the Pictish inhabitants of the MacAlpin state could not live their lives without gaining a knowledge of Gaelic. For the surviving leaders of Pictish society, with a natural wish to perpetuate their status, it was necessary to embrace the language of the court. Like a plant denied sunlight, Pictish withered away, while the Picts lived on as Gaelic speakers. In a land where writing was rare and the oral tradition overwhelmingly important, the accompanying gradual loss of Pictish's content – history, legend, story – was a sad inevitability. Ironically, the steady demise of Pictish from around 900 to 1100 is paralleled by the way in which Gaelic, in turn, yielded to the Scots form of English. The reasons – legal, economic, political, and social – were very similar. Indeed, the decline of Gaelic, which began in the mid-eleventh century, was probably under way before Pictish had quite disappeared from use.

As we have seen in their legend of Pictish origins, the Scots made some efforts to justify their rule over the Picts, which suggests that they felt a need to do so. Perhaps there was a campaign among the scholars to denigrate or ignore Pictish history and legend, of which nothing directly survives. Yet there cannot have been a sustained attack. The most cogent reason for denying any onslaught on Pictish culture by the Scottish rulers is the survival, during that period, of the Pictish symbol stones. Any serious attempt to eradicate a distinctive tradition would have meant the destruction of such works. Neglect and a concentration on the Gaelic tradition in places of learning are more likely to be the reasons. And yet, the degree of Gaelic encroachment was very great. The extent to which Gaels actually took possession of Pictish lands is not clear, but their language certainly did. Few place names survive that can be confidently said to be entirely Pictish. The two distinctive groups of names, those beginning with 'Pit-' (a form unique to Pictland) and with 'Aber-' (a form shared by Pictish and Cumbric), in almost all cases have a Gaelic suffix attached to the Pictish prefix. It has been plausibly suggested that the preservation of 'Pit-' is because it had a legal significance, in land law, which had no exact Gaelic equivalent. The survival of 'Aber-' against Gaelic 'Inver-' may also involve a special application, possibly to do with river junctions or estuaries that had a particular spiritual or cultic importance, conveyed by the Pictish rather than the Gaelic prefix.

The Fight for Bernicia

In the early years of his reign, deployment of Constantine's power and diplomacy was needed to the south. In 910, Edward the Elder, king of Wessex, defeated the York Danes, but the Dublin-based Norwegians moved in quickly and took over not only the kingdom of York but that of Bernicia too, following the defeat of a Bernician army with Scots allies at Corbridge, also in 910. With Bernicia now in the hands of the Norse king Ragnall, Constantine II had a Viking kingdom at his southern frontier. This was less threatening than might seem. Ragnall, his resources heavily stretched between a base at Waterford in Ireland and his York and Bernician domains, found himself struggling between the compact powers of Wessex and of the Scots, who at this time were also strengthening their control of Cumbria, as a southern province of Strathclyde.

In 918, there was another battle with the Norsemen at Corbridge, with the forces of Constantine again allied with Ealdred, the exiled Anglian king of Bernicia. Both sides claimed victory. But Ragnall's position was not weakened, and Constantine retreated. These southern adventures of the Scots, caused probably by the fact that Constantine had obtained promises of subjection from Ealdred, if he were restored and therefore had the southern borders of both Bernicia and Strathclyde to protect, were overshadowed in 920 by the rising power of Wessex-Mercia. In that year, Edward the Elder was able to impose a treaty on both the Scots and the Danes. The

Anglo-Saxon Chronicle interprets this as the kings of the Scots and of Strathclyde, as well as Ragnall and the Anglian Bernicians, accepting Edward 'for father and for lord'. It is a tendentious way of describing the courtesies of what was a peace treaty, though Edward clearly emerges as the strongest party in the negotiations. Sir Frank Stenton's comment is:

> 'To Edward himself the submission meant that each ruler who became his man promised to respect his territory and to attack his enemies. These are simple obligations, and they no more than dimly foreshadow the elaborate feudal relationship which many medieval, and some later, historians have read into them.' (*Anglo-Saxon England*)

Edward's long-term aim was to retrieve the territory once controlled by all the Anglo-Saxon kingdoms, in order to unite them under his own family's imperial crown, and his son, Athelstan, inherited both his purpose and his abilities. There was a crusading element also. The York Vikings were pagans who worshipped and sacrificed to Odin and the other gods of the Old Norse pantheon. A Christian evangelistic quality is plain in the West Saxon attitude, which deprecated the Scots' alliance with such heathen people as these. The more pragmatic Constantine gave shelter to the Viking leader Guthfrith, who had fled from York when Athelstan attacked it in 927. Constantine even married his daughter to Guthfrith's son, Olaf (Athelstan's sister had married Sihtric, king of York, but it is supposed some form of baptism preceded this). What the divines of St Andrews and Dunkeld made of these proceedings is not known. Constantine appears to have had his senior clerics well under control.

On 12 July 927, Constantine, Athelstan, the king of Strathclyde, and the Anglian ruler of Bamburgh met at Eamont, near Penrith, on the Strathclyde border. This conference, held at Athelstan's behest, again is taken by English sources to mean a form of subjection of the king of Scots. Sir Frank Stenton's classic, *Anglo-Saxon England*, repeats: 'the kings of Scotland and Strathclyde . . . became his men'. The *Anglo-Saxon Chronicle* merely says that peace was 'established with pledge and oaths'. Meanwhile, Athelstan took Northumberland into his domain. He now ruled from Winchester to the Firth of Forth. The peace of Eamont lasted for seven years. In 934, Athelstan, citing pledge-breaking by Owen of Strathclyde and by Constantine, mounted a large-scale land and sea attack. His army reached as far as the Mearns, destroying as it went, and his fleet reached as far as Caithness; an attack there suggests that the Norwegian jarldom was in alliance with the Scots. The Scots appear to have retreated before him, following a policy going back to the second century, and there was no great battle.

At the end of the campaigning season, the English retired, leaving a ravaged countryside, but with no recorded gain in terms of territory or tribute. The *Anglo-Saxon Chronicle*, in describing this invasion, for the first time refers to North Britain as Scotland (though the text may not have been written until 975). Also in 934, Guthfrith's son, Olaf, became king of Dublin and, three years later, Anglo-Scottish hostilities resumed. Olaf hoped to regain the kingdom of York. Constantine supported him, both because he feared English hegemony and because a friendly Norse state situated between his kingdom, now assuming the name of Scotia or Scotland, and the assertive power of England, would be no bad thing. The Strathclyders, under their king Owen, either joined in or were summoned. In the autumn of 937, at an unidentified site known from the records as Brunanburh, the Scots' and Norsemen's hopes were crushed in a massive defeat. The king of Strathclyde, whose death is recorded in 937, was probably one of many victims. Constantine escaped by sea. Despite such a major setback, Olaf reinvaded Northumbria on Athelstan's death in 939 and re-established the Viking kingdom without further support from Scotland. His campaign extended north of Tweed, and the rich church of Tyninghame near Dunbar was destroyed.

When Constantine II gave up the kingship and retired to the monastery of Kilrymont in 943, his successor was Malcolm I, son of Donald II. Constantine was already an old man for his era, but he lived on into the next decade. Inevitably the struggle between the Anglo-Saxon and Viking kingdoms went on; neither felt able to tolerate the other and each was occupying territory deemed to be historically the other's. The Scots and Strathclyde were not always able to keep on the sidelines.

After Olaf Guthfrithsson's death, the new king of Dublin, Olaf Cuaran, was ousted from York and retired into the friendly territory of Strathclyde to regroup his forces. The Anglo-Saxon king Edmund invaded Strathclyde with great ferocity and Olaf retreated to Dublin. The king of Strathclyde was Donald, brother of Constantine II. His fate is unclear but his family appears to have paid the penalty for harbouring Olaf. His sons were blinded and thus removed from eligibility as future rulers. The overkingship of Strathclyde was given to Malcolm, Owen's brother, who had become king of Scots in 943, and the Strathclyde kingship was given to Indulf, son of Constantine, who would, in due course, assume the kingship of the Scots on Malcolm's death in 954. While Edmund, in Strathclyde at the head of an army, must have had a prime hand in the dispensations of 945, his range of options was limited. Once again, the centralising trend of the MacAlpins is apparent. From now on, kings would descend either from Constantine II or from Malcolm I. In the following year, Edmund was assassinated and the new Anglo-Saxon king, Eadred, travelled north to receive what the *Anglo-Saxon Chronicle* refers to as the 'customary' pledges from York, Strathclyde, and the Scots. Following Edmund's invasion, it would seem that 'Cumberland', which might mean part or all of Strathclyde in the usage of the time, was held by the king of Scots on the sufferance of the Anglo-Saxon king. In 946, however, the York leaders invited in a dynamic figure, Erik Bloodaxe, a royal exile from Norway, who had already imposed his own rule on the jarldom of Orkney.

The Scots appear to have remained in alliance with king Olaf Cuaran of the Dublin dynasty, now ousted from York. Between 947 and 954, both the Scots and the Anglo-Saxons struggled to oust Erik, for different reasons: the former to help their ally, the latter to gain control. The 'Scottish Chronicle' record of Malcolm's foray into Northumberland of 948–49, that he 'plundered the English to the River Tees', suggests, as indeed was likely, that a substantial Anglian population continued to live in the disputed Norse-controlled land between the Firth of Forth and the Tees. In 952, Eadred secured control of York and, in 954, Erik Bloodaxe was killed.

The so-called *Prophecy of Berchán*, written in the late eleventh century, praises Constantine:

'Alba was brimful from his day,
His was the long fair reign . . .
With ale, with music, with fellowship,
With corn, with milk, with active kine,
With pride, with success, with elegance.'

Longevity always enhances a reign in the eyes of those who look back, and Constantine II had a reign of remarkable length. He had real achievements to look back on. Brunanburh was a disaster but not a catastrophe and, even if the battle had gone the other way, it would have been unlikely to impede the ultimate rise of the Anglo-Saxon kingdom. In his time, the Scottish kingship grew stronger and its external policy was shrewd and sensible. Despite the tendentious phraseology of the *Anglo-Saxon Chronicle*, there is nothing detectable in his dealings with Athelstan or Eadred to suggest that he was a client-king. In this reign, one can see the start of that centuries-long process, blending at various times appeasement, aggression, friendship, and dissimulation, by which the Scottish kingdom struggled to preserve its integrity against its powerful, intrusive, and often unscrupulous neighbour-state. Internally,

the hold of the MacAlpin dynasty continued to be strength-
ened. The roles of those outside the MacAlpin line of paternal
descent, whose predecessors or forebears had been subkings,
were now beginning to be defined in definitely nonregal terms,
as *mormaers*, a title now generally accepted as meaning 'great
steward'. While the mormaership might be a hereditary post,
its clear implication was as that of a subject, answerable to the
king. It was a different relationship from that of the subking
and overking in former centuries; now the effective power of
the overking was far greater.

Another sign of divergence from both Gaelic and Pictish tradition is found in the naming of Constantine II's elder
son, Indulf: a Norse name. Various things can be read into this,
perhaps too many (perhaps it simply means that his mother
was Norwegian). In some parts of Scotland and Strathclyde,
there were many inhabitants of Norse extraction. Norse kings
still controlled much of Ireland and the Hebrides, and Norway
had resumed possession of the northern isles and the north
mainland. A Norse name for a Scots prince might indicate a
friendly connection with one of the several Norse powers, or
might be part of laying the ground for a territorial claim.

Struggles in the North

From the reign of Malcolm I, a renewed interest in the north
is certainly detectable. He is said to have led an expedition
north of the Mounth, and to have killed Cellach, subking of
Moray. In 954, he was himself killed in battle, at Fetteresso in
Aberdeenshire, by the men of Moerne, or the Mearns, which
suggests that the death of Cellach had not ensured the peace or
loyalty of the province. Between these events, Malcolm also
led his army south into Northumbria. In 949, Olaf Cuaran
made a further attempt to regain the kingdom of York, and the
Scots invasion was undertaken to support him. Traditionally
this invasion was led by the aged Constantine II, emerged

from his monastery for a brief resumption of his kingship. This may just be a story designed to preserve Malcolm from the stigma of breaking his pact with Edmund, which had no doubt been reiterated with Eadred in 946. Olaf retained possession of Northumbria until 954, when Eadred advanced from York and sent him in retreat to Dublin. Northumbria became an Anglo-Saxon earldom.

His name did not spare Indulf from doing battle with Norsemen. He may have been another king who died fighting them, in his case at a site known as Innerculen, probably Cullen in Banffshire, in 962. His death is not noted in the 'Pictish Chronicle', and the eleventh-century *Prophecy of Berchàn* says he died in monastic retirement (Mitchell, 157).

The jarls of Orkney, including Einar and his son, Thorfinn Skull-Splitter, made strenuous efforts to capture the fertile, grain-growing Laigh of Moray, and clearly it was an enormous struggle to hold them back. Conflicts with the Vikings, often organised in bands of *sumarlidi*, or 'summer wanderers', leaving their Orkney farms for a kind of raiding tour down the coast, would continue. But the Norse jarls were becoming increasingly Gaelicised, or, more correctly, in this region, Picticised. Thorfinn Skull-Splitter, who died around 963, married a daughter of Dungadr, or Dungal, the Pictish mormaer whose name is still preserved in that of Duncansby Head. One of their five sons, Skuli, is recorded in the Norse *Book of Flatey* as having received the earldom of Caithness from the Scottish king. He was opposed and killed by his brother, Liotr, who took possession of his domains. Caithness was then invaded by a Scottish mormaer, and a battle was fought at the Skitten Mire, near Watten, which was won by Liotr, who, however, died of his wounds. Though the process would not have been apparent to the mormaers and jarls, who struggled for possession of these windswept moors and cliff-bound coasts, the ill-recorded events reveal the way in which the northern isles and their rulers would always, eventually, be pulled into the Scottish orbit. It seems likely that, although the Norse udal law of land-holding was introduced to the Northern Isles, it was not extended to Norse possessions on the mainland, whose land-holders must have abided by the prevailing system. For three generations, the pattern continued of Norse or part-Norse earls owing theoretical allegiance for their mainland holding to the Scottish king. Skuli was followed by his brother, Hlodvar, who died around 980 and was succeeded by his son Sigurd 'the Stout'. In addition to Orkney, Sigurd assumed the earldom of Caithness as the great-grandson of Dungadr.

According to the *Orkneyinga Saga*, written in 1225, Sigurd's possession of Caithness was challenged by Finnlaec, the mormaer of Moray, who was repulsed by Sigurd's forces at the Skitten Mire, which appears to have been a sort of *champ de Mars* for northern combats. It features again in another battle, fought in Sigurd's absence, when another invasion was mounted by Hundi (this offensive Norse designation has been tentatively identified with Crinan of Dunkeld) and the Pictish-named Maelsnechtan. On this occasion, the Scots prevailed and Sigurd appears to have accepted Scottish overlordship for his Caithness possessions from then on.

If the Norse inhabitants of Caithness and Sutherland were not already Christian, most who were still pagan are likely to have conformed following the celebrated confrontation in Orkney in 997 between king Olaf Tryggvason and jarl Sigurd. As related in the *Orkneyinga Saga*, the king, himself a new convert, said: 'I want you and your subjects to be baptised. If you refuse, I'll have you killed on the spot, and I swear I'll ravage every island with fire and steel.' Prudently, Sigurd accepted conversion, but it is likely that many Norse communities had already abandoned paganism.

The Taking of Lothian

A significant event in the mid-tenth century, with great implications for the future, was the occupation by the Scots of the fortress rock of Din Eiddyn in Lothian, once a strong point of the Cumbric kingdom of Manau Gododdin. For many generations, Lothian had been under Anglian or Norse rule. It had never been a dominion either of the Picts or of the Scots. This happened in 954, after the collapse of Viking rule at York, and while the Anglo-Saxons were fully occupied in establishing their control in the south of the great Northumbrian province. The Scots had every reason to covet Lothian. It had rich farmlands on the coast, as the two Berwicks (Old English *bere wic*, 'barley farm') attest. It was a strategic invasion route from the south, with no significant natural barrier after the Tweed. At least during periods of Norse rule there, it is highly likely that the king of Scots had exercised an overkingship over the area. Now that the old order was shattered, it was prudent rather than opportunistic to take control before the Anglo-Saxons arrived in force to exercise a claim of their own. The 'Pictish Chronicle' states that the fortress was evacuated and abandoned by the Angles, which suggests a siege by the Scots. Many Lothian places were named, or renamed, in Gaelic around this time, following land grants to Scottish settlers, but the Anglian language of the inhabitants was not eliminated, surviving as the origin of the later Scots speech.

Indulf's death or retirement in 962 marked an end to the orderly system of transition between the kingships of Strathclyde and of the Scots, shared between the families of Aed and Malcolm I. His successor, Dub, the son of Malcolm I, was challenged by Indulf's son, Culen. There was civil war between the factions, with a battle fought at Drumcrub in Strathearn, and Dub eventually took refuge in Moray, where he was assassinated. There is a sense here of the provinces of the kingdom moving apart in their allegiances. Culen's support came from Atholl, once a subkingdom, its chief referred to somewhat strangely in the chroniclers' usage, as a *satrapas*, as though he were a magnate under Cyrus of Persia. The ruler of Moray seems to have been playing his own game. In Strathclyde, the king was Donald, son of Owen, whose position (as A. P. Smyth points out) is anomalous in the usual alternation system. Donald assumed the kingship of Strathclyde after Indulf 'stepped up' to Scone in 954. The fact that he called his son by the Brittonic name of Rhyderch again suggests a separatist tendency. In the mid-tenth century there was a real prospect that the MacAlpin kingdom might disintegrate into warring provinces.

Culen assumed the kingship of Scots in 966, on the killing of Dub. This settled nothing; warfare continued and, in 971, he and his brother, Eochaid, were killed in Lothian, fighting the men of Strathclyde under Rhyderch (the kingdom of Strathclyde, too, could exercise a historic claim on this formerly Cumbric-speaking territory). Kenneth II, brother of Dub, then became king of Scots, probably controlling little more than Strathearn and Fife, and facing armed opposition both from Culen's brother, Olaf, and from Strathclyde. Olaf was finally killed in 977. Fighting continued in Lothian, with the Strathclyde men being victors in a pitched battle at Abercorn in the early part of the reign. The Fords of Frew, the first crossing point on the Forth, west of Stirling, were fortified by the Scots; at this time, evidently, their overkingship of Strathclyde had little practical meaning. But it appears that Kenneth II gradually imposed himself. Four generations away from his eponymous ancestor and founder of the dynasty, he was another strongman with similar qualities of military leadership and of political skill. And, not least, he took close heed of the means of nurturing what one might almost call the family business – keeping and extending centralised power. Even before internal opposition had been put down, he was strong enough to mount an invasion of Northumbria, as far south as Cleveland.

Relations with the English

In a famous verbal snapshot, recorded by Aelfric, abbot of Eynsham, the recently crowned English king Edgar is seen in

973, at Chester, being rowed on the River Dee by a group of eight kings and subkings from within the British Isles. These included Kenneth II, king of Scots, and Malcolm, king of the Cumbrians. Aelfric said they had come to acknowledge Edgar's supremacy. Inevitably this has been seen by English historians as a form of homage, though with no evidence to say what form of homage, or what for. At this time, Kenneth had secured his position as king of Scots and was master of the old Bernicia. Malcolm, whatever his position with reference to Kenneth, was king of a resurgent Strathclyde that encompassed Gaels and Norse, as well as its residual Brittonic population, and that reached as far south as the Stainmore Pass in the Pennines. The pre-eminence in wealth, manpower, and land of the English king was obvious, but that does not turn the others into client-kings. The gathering at Chester was a tenth-century form of the 'summit meeting', of a more celebratory kind than the one at Eamont between Constantine and Athelstan. There was much for the rulers to discuss, with boundaries and zones of influence still in dispute. A further visit by Kenneth II to Edgar is recorded by the 13th-century English historian, Roger of Wendover, who says that, on this occasion, Edgar ceded the territory of Lothian to Kenneth, together with certain manors in England to support him financially on further visits to London. Roger also says that Kenneth did homage to Edgar, but for what is not stated.

Kenneth II died in 995; his end is accounted for in Irish sources as assassination by 'his own people' and in later Scottish ones as through a treacherous ambush near Fettercairn set up by Finbhalla, daughter of the mormaer of Angus. Kenneth had had cause to execute her son, with a blood feud being the result, though it is likely that the enmity had been present for a long time. The medieval chronicler Andrew of Wyntoun recorded:

> 'As through the Mernys on a day
> The king was rydand his hey way;
> Off his awyne curt al suddanly

Agayne him ras a cumpany
Into the town of Fetherkerne.'

With Kenneth's strong personality removed from the scene, faction struggles broke out again. He was succeeded by Constantine III, known as 'the Bald', who was killed in internal strife only two years later. The son of Culen, he was the last of the descendants of Kenneth MacAlpin's son, Aed, to become king. Kenneth III, son of Dub, was crowned at Scone; as Dub had been dead for 31 years, this Kenneth may already have been elderly and his son Giric may have ruled jointly with him. In the 'Scottish Chronicle', Giric is recorded as having reigned alone. During this period, the Scots appear to have fought off an invasion of Cumbria under the English king Aethelred, which suggests that any separatist urge in Strathclyde itself had been checked either by external pressure from the south or by a victory for the Scots. But in 1005, amidst continuing internal warfare, both Kenneth III and Giric were killed in battle, at Monzievaird in Strathearn, by the supporters of Kenneth II's elder son Malcolm, who became king as Malcolm II. From now on, with one notable exception, the kings would descend in direct line from him until the death of Alexander III in 1286. But it may be noted that Kenneth III's son, Boite, had a daughter, Gruoch, who married Macbeth, mormaer of Moray, as her second husband. The other families with claims to the kingship did not subscribe to the monopoly now being exercised, and there would be trouble to come.

High Kings and Dynastic Marriages

Malcolm II's reign was a lengthy one and, during its course, the wider political scene in the British Isles changed dramatically. In Ireland, the emergence in 1002 of Brian Bòruma, 'tribute gainer', as high king had instituted a central rule, albeit a disputed one, and put the Dublin Norse kingdom, now under king Sihtric Silkbeard, the son of Olaf Cuaran, under great pressure. Ireland could no longer be ignored as a patchwork of discordant petty kingdoms, but had to be viewed as a significant power. Malcolm's wife was, however, a 'woman of Leinster' and Leinster was home of the native opposition to Brian; friendly relations between the king of Scots and the new high king were unlikely.

In 1006, it seems likely that Malcolm II made an unsuccessful invasion of Bernicia and was forced back from a siege of Durham; reading from English chronicles, Sir Frank Stenton, in *Anglo-Saxon England*, says the heir apparent to the Northumberland earldom, Uhtred, 'annihilated the Scottish army in a battle of which a vivid memory survived the Norman Conquest' (Stenton, 418). Certainly, Malcolm II did not try his luck to the south for some years after that, though he had much to occupy him in his own kingdom. The resurgence of Danish power under king Sweyn brought frequent attacks and land invasions. Moray was invaded, and battles were fought as far inland as Mortlach, where Malcolm is recorded as having won a victory in 1010, turning back Norse invaders who had forced their way far up the Spey valley. In this he may have been supported by Sigurd, jarl of Orkney and Caithness. Another Norse invasion was repulsed at Barry, at the mouth of the Firth of Tay.

In 1014, a great battle was fought at Clontarf, outside Dublin, where two armies met, both composed of mixed elements of Norsemen and Irishmen. One was Brian Bòruma's; the other was Sihtric's. Brian's force won the day, though the high king himself was killed. It was the effective end of Norse power in Ireland, though not of the Norse presence there; but also the end of Brian's ambition of achieving for his family in Ireland what the MacAlpins had done in Scotland. Though the Scottish king was not involved in the battle or the power struggle which preceded it, men from the old Pictland fought on Brian's side, under the mormaer of Mar, who was killed. Men from Orkney and other Norse areas fought for Sihtric under the leadership of Sigurd the Stout, jarl of Orkney and Caithness, who was also killed. The Scots took advantage of this fall in the Norsemen's fortunes in the west, and the *Prophecy of Berchán* records a campaign by Malcolm II in the southern Hebrides, when it hails him as 'Danger of Britons, Extinction of Galls, Mariner of Ile and Arann'. Critical developments were also occurring in southern England where Danish raids were building up in force and frequency. In 1016, the English king, Aethelred, died, even as Sweyn's son, Cnut, brother of king Harold of Denmark, was about to lay siege to London. By the end of the year, Cnut was undisputed master of England. In the north, the veteran Norwegian warrior, Erik of Hlathir, was made earl of Northumberland.

Malcolm II had daughters, but no son, or none who survived. One daughter, Bethoc, was given as wife to Crinan, the lay abbot of Dunkeld, a title that signifies that Crinan, a nobleman who had not taken holy orders, held the lands and revenues of the monastery, and took responsibility for maintaining its religious functions through a prior. Another daughter was married to Sigurd, jarl of Orkney and Caithness, who was killed at Clontarf. Later accounts also say a daughter – or sister – of Malcolm's was married to Finnlaec, mormaer of Moray. There is no real evidence for this, though Finnlaec, around 1005, became the father of Macbeth, and such a marriage would fully justify Macbeth's eventual claim to the throne. These were purposeful dispensations by the king. Malcolm did not intend his lack of sons to stand in the way of his family's continuing supremacy. Diplomatic marriages by no means always worked, in the diplomatic sense, but they show a willingness on both sides to behave in a friendly way. For Malcolm II, Sigurd's friendliness meant that the old Pictish northeast, with its disaffected and ambitious mormaers, was isolated. With Finnlaec as a son-in-law, some of the stress between north and south might be removed. Malcolm II had no intention of preferring the Moray family, however, and nor did he intend to make Crinan the next king; his eye was on his grandson, Crinan's son, Duncan. In due course, Duncan became king of Strathclyde, either because the line stemming from Owen had no candidate after the death of Owen the Bald in 1018, or because he was simply imposed. His brother Maldred, who married a daughter of the Anglo-Saxon earl of Northumberland, Uhtred, appears to have had possessions in Cumberland, suggesting that the kingdom may have been divided between them, or that, as had happened before, Cumberland was ruled as a subkingdom or province of Strathclyde.

The status of the Norse possessions in the northern mainland had varied, depending on political conditions in the Vikings' own world. The Norse jarls, increasingly Norse-Gaelic in their culture and political interests, found it useful to play off the Scottish king against their Norwegian overlord. The Pictish-Scottish kingdom had never relinquished its claim to the Viking-occupied region and both sides had co-existed for more than 100 years in an uneasy relationship, with periods of warfare and sporadic raids between spells of relative peace. The brunt of confrontation was borne by the people of Moray (which extended into the present Inverness district) and the mormaer of Moray often made war or peace without the sanction of the king of Scots. (In the 'Annals of Ulster', Finnlaec, the father of Macbeth, and other rulers of Moray, are referred to as *ri Alban*, 'king of Alba'). The internal affairs of that province were turbulent. Finnlaec was killed by his nephews in 1020; one of these was Gillecomghain, Gruoch's first husband, who was mormaer when he was burned to death in 1029. The burning of Dunkeld is recorded in that same year; accidental fires were common enough, but Dunkeld, Crinan's stronghold, was out on the northern edge of safe territory and vulnerable to raids from beyond the mountains.

After Clontarf, Sigurd's three elder sons by a previous marriage divided the northern isles among themselves. His youngest son, five-year-old Thorfinn, grandson of Malcolm II and first cousin to Duncan and perhaps to Macbeth, was named as the earl of Caithness. The *Orkneyinga Saga*, written down around 1225, records that Malcolm 'bestowed Caithness and Sutherland on him with the title of earl, and gave him men to rule the domain along with him.' The saga records that when king Olaf of Norway later demanded Thorfinn's fealty, the jarl replied that he was already pledged to the king of Scots.

If Malcolm II had hoped in this way to bind the far-north earldom more closely to the Scottish crown, the wish was not to be realised. In manhood, Thorfinn became jarl of Orkney as well as Caithness, and showed every sign of vigorous independence. 'Everyone could see he was going to turn out greedy,' remarked the saga-writer. In 1029–3, he was campaigning in the north, winning a battle, probably on the Tarbet peninsula in Easter Ross, against a mormaer referred to in the *Orkneyinga Saga* as Karl Hundason, 'son of a dog', possibly a derogatory epithet for Macbeth. It was in the aftermath of a failed campaign against his half-Norse cousin, Thorfinn, that Duncan himself would be killed by Macbeth in 1040, and Macbeth would take over the kingship.

The Holding of Lothian

After 1014, Malcolm II could reasonably think he had resolved the problem of the Viking north, with himself as its overlord, and his own men as tutors to the boy-jarl of Caithness. The troublesome province of Moray had been isolated. To the west, he still had Gall-Gaidhill sea kings and their piratical power bases, but his Islay and Arran campaigns might have tamed them somewhat. A major challenge, however, still faced him to the south, where the Danish Cnut was firmly established as king of England. The king of Scots was in possession of Lothian, but also kept up an acquisitive interest in the lands to the south of Cheviot. The earldom of Northumberland included old Bernicia. To Malcolm II, Bernicia was a province that, following the long overlordship of Constantine, rightly belonged to him.

On the other hand, quite apart from the fact that Anglo-Saxon possession of Northumberland had brought it into the English area of influence, Cnut, as a Dane, would be well aware of earlier Danish involvement there. Any Scottish claim would be contested. In 1018, Malcolm II invaded Bernicia to assert his rights, supported by a Strathclyde army under its king Owen the Bald. At Carham, just south of the Tweed, a battle was fought, resulting in a complete victory for the Scots and their allies.

The importance of Carham, its date, and the leadership of Cnut's English army there, have been much debated. The last two points revolve around whether Cnut had the Anglo-Saxon earl Uhtred executed in 1016 or 1018, and thus whether Uhtred could have led the English forces at Carham. The chronicle sources give contradictory accounts but, for Scottish history, the prime point is the political significance of what was certainly a major victory in strict military terms. The English chronicler, Symeon of Durham says that, after Carham, the earl yielded up to Scotland 'the whole of Lodoneia [Lothian] in satisfaction of their claim and for a solid peace. In this manner Lodoneia was annexed to the kingdom of the Scots.' Earlier historians tended to follow Symeon's account, but as we have seen, another source places the formal acquisition of Lothian firmly in the reign of Kenneth II. Stenton, who tends to report events from the English regal viewpoint, though always most fairly, states:

> ' . . . there is no evidence for the view that it was the defeat at Carham which led to the acquisition of Lothian by the Scots. According to Symeon, the English army was drawn from the country between the Tees and the Tweed, a description which suggests . . . that the English boundary had already been withdrawn from the latter river.'

A. A. M. Duncan suggests that the heavy Scottish defeat at Durham in 1006 may have resulted in the loss of some or all the territory of Lothian, which seems a reasonable hypothesis.

The permanent loss of this rich province might not have prevented the survival of a unified Scotland, but it would certainly have meant a very different future. If the Scots had been defeated at Carham, the loss of Lothian might have been formalised. What Carham did was to remove any risk of such a thing, to retrieve any lost ground, and to place Malcolm II's marker very strongly on Bernicia.

Thirteen years later, in 1031, Cnut himself came north, despite the many demands of his multinational North Sea empire, and entered Scotland with an army, reaching as far as Abernethy. It is likely that Malcolm II was playing North Sea politics himself – at this time the Norwegians were in rebellion against Cnut's rule, with jarl Thorfinn's nephew, Ragnvald, playing a major part – and this, rather than the disputed suzerainty of Bernicia, may have caused the armed visit, which ended in Malcolm's submission to Cnut. Since all submissions of kings of Scots to kings of England are contentious matters, it is as well to state that, at this time, a submission was still of a personal nature. It would have bound Malcolm to be Cnut's man, and to assist him in his ventures and to refrain from assisting his enemies. There is no reason to suppose that it gave Cnut any rights over the Scottish kingdom and, even if it had, these would have died with him.

A Single Kingdom

Malcolm II died in 1034, peacefully, as far as is known. He was the last king in direct male descent from Kenneth MacAlpin, and the first to be referred to – by the Irish chronicler Marianus Scotus – as king of Scotia (Marianus's by-name still meant 'Irishman' at this time: the term 'Scot' was still in flux, though increasingly acquiring its modern meaning). His sister's son, Duncan – who is described in the *Prophecy of St Berchán* as *Ilgalrach*, 'the much-diseased' – was installed at Scone as king of Scots, with the support of his father, Crinan, and in despite of his relatives in Moray. A new constitutional departure accompanied this event. No one replaced Duncan as king of Strathclyde. Perhaps this was because there was no candidate considered reliable – the obvious ones were from the Moray family – or perhaps it was no longer considered necessary. Strathclyde was assumed into Scotland (in the next century, under Alexander I, it appears to have become semidetached again for a time, assigned to his brother David, though not as a kingdom). Cumbria, to its south, perhaps already governed separately by Maldred, was soon to be incorporated into England by earl Siward of Northumberland, who would also deny Bernicia to the Scots.

Malcolm II had made his dispensations as well as he could and in accordance with the tradition of the house of Alpin. These appear to have included the killing of the young son or grandson of Boite, son of Kenneth III, recorded by a chronicler as having his brains dashed out. But in the marriages of his daughters lay the seeds of discord to come. This became all the more inevitable on the marriage of Macbeth to Gruoch, granddaughter of Kenneth III. Gruoch had just as much claim as Bethoc to be the woman whose sons should continue the royal line. The old tradition of the *derbfine* was in tatters by now but, for any traditionalist, she was well within the magic circle. Macbeth, as a hereditary mormaer, possibly of royal blood, possessed at least as much status as Crinan. The Moray family also harboured a further claimant, with more justification than Macbeth. Gruoch had had a son by her first husband Gillecomghain (also, perhaps, a descendant of Kenneth III), named Lulach, to whom Macbeth was stepfather. Lulach would be recognised in the north as king of Scots, after Macbeth's death, until he died a year later, fighting his cousin, Malcolm III, Duncan's son, in Strathbogie. All this and much more lay ahead, but none of it was to set aside the fact that, with the peaceful accession of Duncan, Scotland had emerged as a single kingdom, one of the first unified states in modern Europe. The integrity of the kingdom would always survive.

Bibliography

Anderson, A. O. *Scottish Annals from English Chronicles AD 500–1280*. London 1988

Anderson, Marjorie, *Kings and Kingship in Early Scotland*. Edinburgh, 1973

Chadwick, H. M., *Early Scotland*. Cambridge, 1949

Chadwick, Nora, *The Celts*. New edition, London, 1997

Cunliffe, Barry, *The Ancient Celts*. Oxford, 1981

Duncan, A. A. M., *Scotland: The Making of the Kingdom*. Edinburgh 1975

Feachem, Richard, *The North Britons*. London, 1965

Foster, Sally, *Picts, Gaels and Scots*. London, 1996

Frere, Sheppard, *Britannia*. London, 1987

Henderson, Isabel, *The Picts*. London, 1967

Hughes, Kathleen, Celtic Britain in the Early Middle Ages. Woodbridge, 1986

MacKillop, James, *Dictionary of Celtic Mythology*. Oxford, 1998

Meldrum, E. (ed.), *The Dark Ages in the Highlands*. Inverness, 1971

Mitchell, Dugald, *History of the Highlands and Gaelic Scotland*. Paisley, 1900

Nicolaisen, Bill, *The Picts and their Place Names*. Rosemarkie, 1996

Piggott, Stuart, *Scotland Before History*. London, 1958

Roberts, J. L., *Lost Kingdoms*. Edinburgh, 1997

Ross, Anne, *Pagan Celtic Britain*. London, 1967

Ross, Anne, *The Druids*. Stroud, 1999

Salway, Peter, *Roman Britain*. Oxford, 1981

Scott Moncrieff, G. (ed.), *The Stones of Scotland*. London, 1938

Skene, W. F., *Chronicles of the Picts and Scots*. Edinburgh, 1867

Skene, W. F., *Celtic Scotland, Vols 1–3*. Edinburgh, 1886–90

Smyth, A. P., *Warlords and Holy Men*. London, 1984

Stenton, Sir Frank, *Anglo-Saxon England*. Oxford, 1971

Watson, W. J., *History of the Celtic Place Names of Scotland*. Edinburgh, 1926

Transactions of the Gaelic Society of Inverness